A SHORT HISTORY
OF THE SCOTTISH DRESS

CHILDREN OF FREDERICK, PRINCE OF WALES By Du Pan

This painting shows George III (second from the right) as a boy in the uniform of the Royal Company of Archers.

A SHORT HISTORY
OF THE
SCOTTISH
DRESS

R. M. D. GRANGE

LONDON
BURKE'S PEERAGE LIMITED

*Set in 14 on 16 pt Bembo, the text and black and white illus-
trations in this book have been printed by offset lithography on
Mellotex Matt High White Cartridge. The full colour art
plates have been printed by letterpress on Invercarron White
Art and the book has been bound in Sundour Art Buckram*

This book has been printed and bound in England by William
Clowes and Sons Limited, London and Beccles for the publishers,
Burke's Peerage Limited (registered office: 180 Fleet Street,
London, E.C.4), publishing offices: Mercury House, Waterloo
Road, London, S.E.1

MADE AND PRINTED IN GREAT BRITAIN

TO

J. M. RIVERS

who helped such a lot

Acknowledgments

IN PARTICULAR, I would like to thank Sir Iain Moncreiffe of that Ilk, Bt., who read the typescript and offered valuable advice.

In addition, I wish to thank Sir Thomas Innes of Learney, the Lord Lyon King of Arms, who suggested in the first place that the book should be published.

Thanks are also due to Mr R. E. Hutchison, Keeper, National Portrait Gallery of Scotland, Mr B. Skinner of the National Portrait Gallery of Scotland, Mr W. Y. Carman, Keeper of Exhibits, Imperial War Museum, London, and to Mr Peter Townend, Editor, *Burke's Peerage, Baronetage and Knightage*, who kindly supplied me with information.

I am also indebted to Mr M. F. R. Cory who prepared two of the illustrations for the book, and to Mr Tom Scott, who photographed a number of the portraits, including some of those in colour.

Contents

	page
ACKNOWLEDGMENTS	ix
LIST OF ILLUSTRATIONS	xvii
PROLOGUE	xxvii
FOREWORD	xxxi
PUBLISHER'S NOTE	xxxv

Chapter One

EARLY TIMES — 3

Chapter Two

THE SAFFRON TUNIC AND
THE TARTAN PLAID — 19

Chapter Three

THE BELTED PLAID AND THE
SOMBRE BROADCLOTH — 37

Chapter Four

TARTAN—THE SYMBOL OF SCOTLAND — 65

A SHORT ANTHOLOGY — 103

BIBLIOGRAPHY — 115

INDEX OF SOURCES — 119

List of Illustrations

CHILDREN OF FREDERICK, PRINCE OF WALES By Du Pan

This painting shows George III as a boy in the uniform of the Royal Company of Archers. He was brought up under the care of the Earl of Bute

Reproduced by gracious permission of Her Majesty the Queen   frontispiece

THE LAIRD OF CLUNY-MACPHERSON (Artist unknown)

This picture shows the plaid being worn with trews, popular with chieftains and others for winter wear

Courtesy: Scottish National Portrait Gallery   5

MAP OF SCOTLAND By John Speed (1552–1629)

This map is interesting as it illustrates well the more primitive form of the dress and is one of the earliest pictures showing tartan

Courtesy: Trustees of the National Library of Scotland   8 and 9

FALKIRK TARTAN (a)

During levelling operations in Bell's Meadow, north of Callender Park, a workman struck a jar which cracked. Its mouth was filled with this piece of cloth and the jar contained coins dating from 83 B.C. to A.D. 230. There were more than 1,925 in number

Courtesy: National Museum of Antiquities of Scotland   10

FALKIRK TARTAN (b)

'The Falkirk twill is certainly the earliest herringbone recorded for Scotland, and the earliest tartan, too, if we may claim it as such on the strength of the stripes and checks . . . a poor man's plaid with two colours only, dark and light brown.' *Two Textiles from the National Museum, Edinburgh* by Mrs G. M. Crowfoot

Courtesy: National Museum of Antiquities of Scotland   11

HIGHLAND GRAVE SLAB

'The armour of the knightly effigies found in the West Highlands is a most puzzling affair. One thing I have not found at any place which I have visited— what we now term the Highland Dress.' James Drummond in *The Sculptured Monuments in Iona and the West Highlands*

Courtesy: Dundalgan Press (W. Tempest) Limited   13

FIFTEENTH-CENTURY CORBEL IN THE ABBEY KIRK, PAISLEY

This corbel depicts a young man wearing a short, kilted tunic, very much like a modern kilt

Courtesy: Edinburgh University Press and the Ministry of Public Building and Works from 'The Mediaeval Stone Carver in Scotland' by James S. Richardson   14

DOCTOR NATHANIEL SPENS By Sir Henry Raeburn, 1791

Dr Spens is wearing the uniform of the Royal Company of Archers

Courtesy: Captain-General and Council of The Queen's Body Guard for Scotland, Royal Company of Archers   facing 16

TULLOCH OF DUNBENNAN, THE JACOBITE

The sitter wears a tartan coat, a plaid draped over his left shoulder and a dark bonnet

Courtesy: Sir Thomas Innes of Learney, K.C.V.O., the Lord Lyon King of Arms   22

FRANCIS CHARTERIS, 7TH EARL OF WEMYSS By Allan Ramsay

The Laird of Wemyss lived in Lowland Fife. He held some lands in the Highlands. The picture was painted in 1745

Courtesy: The Rt. Hon. the Earl of Wemyss and March, K.T.   23

SIR ARCHIBALD BURNETT OF CARLOPS By Richard Wait

He was admitted to the Royal Company of Archers in 1708 and wears a red tartan

Courtesy: Captain-General and Council of The Queen's Body Guard for Scotland, Royal Company of Archers   facing 24

SCOTS IN PARIS, 1562

These pictures are from a French book called *Receuil de la Diversité des Habits* published in Paris in 1562

Courtesy: Bodleian Library   25

FLORA MACDONALD (1722–1790) By Allan Ramsay

She helped Prince Charles Edward to escape to Skye. She was arrested and imprisoned but was later released

Courtesy: Bodleian Library   28

HIGH BOOTS

'They go barehead, and let their hair grow very long, and wear neither hose nor shoes, except some who have boots made in an old-fashioned way, which come as high as their knees.' Nicolay d'Arfeville, 1583

Courtesy: M. Cory   31

ALEXANDER ROBERTSON OF BROWNSBANK, PRENDERGUEST
AND GUNSGREEN IN THE COUNTY OF BERWICK 1748–1804
By William Mosman

This portrait was painted when he was six years old in 1754, during the proscription of tartan

Courtesy: Sheriff A. M. Prain   32

JAMES, 5TH EARL OF WEMYSS *c.* 1715

In the uniform of the Royal Company of Archers. The tartan was later
changed to a green sett

Courtesy: Captain-General and Council of The Queen's Body Guard for Scotland,
Royal Company of Archers   facing 34

JOHN STUART, 3RD EARL OF BUTE (1713–1792) In the collection of
the Marquess of Bute (probably by William Aikman *c.* 1730)

This form of the dress was favoured by the nobility

Courtesy: The Marquess of Bute   38

GERMAN WOODCUT, 1631

Although described as Irish, these are really Scottish soldiers, probably of
Mackay's Regiment who took part in the capture of Stettin in 1630

Courtesy: Trustees of the British Museum   41

THE ARMS OF THE BURNETTS OF LEYS Granted 21 April 1626

In 1659 Sir George MacKenzie published a book on heraldry. In it he refers to
the supporter of the above arms as 'a Highlander in Hunting Garb'. The
illustration is taken from the Coat of Arms in plaster at Muchalls in Kincardineshire which was finished about 1627   44

HIGHLAND CHIEFTAIN By Michael Wright, *c.* 1660

This portrait is most probably that of 'Lacey the Actor' dressed as a Highland
chief. The costume would certainly be too flamboyant for most Highlanders
of that time

Courtesy: Scottish National Portrait Gallery   45

From MAP OF ABERDEEN, 1661 By James Gordon of Rothiemay (1615–1686)

Gordon's *Map of Aberdeen* shows a figure of what appears to be a boy wearing
a kilt. He gave a detailed description of the dress in his *History of Scots Affair*,
explaining several ways in which the plaid could be worn. He does mention
one way as 'folded all round the body about the region of the belt'

Courtesy: Trustees of the British Museum   46

7TH EARL OF ARGYLL, Justice-General of Scotland. Died 1638

Although not clear from this reproduction, the figure is wearing tartan ribbons at the neck and the garters. He is in Spanish uniform, having entered the service of Philip III of Spain

Courtesy: His Grace the Duke of Argyll　　　　47

LORD DUFFUS (1670–1750) By Richard Wait

Thomas Kirk describes such a dress in 1678 'The Highlanders wear slashed doublets, commonly without breeches, only a plad tyed about their wastes, etc., thrown over their shoulders'

Courtesy: Scottish National Portrait Gallery　　　　51

THE BELTED PLAID By Sir David Wilkie

This very fine drawing shows the dress of the poorest Highlander. It consists solely of a plaid forming the complete dress, leaving the legs and an arm bare

Courtesy: Captain and Mrs Bruce Ingram　　　　53

4TH DUKE OF PERTH

The tartans worn are not the same as those worn by the Third Duke shown on page 59

Courtesy: The Rt. Hon. the Earl of Ancaster　　　　57

3RD DUKE OF PERTH (1713–1746) By F. de Troy

He died on his way to France after the battle of Culloden. He wears the plaid with tartan trews, a form of the costume favoured more by the nobility at that time. The tartans do not correspond with those in the portrait of the Fourth Duke of Perth, shown on page 57

Courtesy: The Rt. Hon. the Earl of Ancaster　　　　59

CUARANS

'The shoes antiently wore, were a piece of the hide of a deer, cow or horse, with the hair on, being tied behind and before with a point of leather.' Martin Martin's *Western Isles*, 1703

Courtesy: M. Cory　　　　61

JAMES MORAY OF ABERCAIRNY (1705–1777) By Jeremiah Davison, c. 1739

This is an excellent picture showing the belted plaid, the 'kilt' being the lower part of the plaid. The tartans are unknown today and different from those in the picture on page 73

Courtesy: Major James Drummond Moray　　　　facing 62

HALKERSTON OF RATHILLET IN FIFE (Artist unknown)

He wears a coat and plaid of tartans unknown today. His bonnet bears the Jacobite white cockade. This portrait was painted soon after the Rebellion of 1745

Courtesy: Mrs Macqueen Ferguson 66

ARCHERY MEDALS (a) Alexander MacLeod of Muiravonside, 1735; (b) Alexander Bayne of Rirachies, 1745; (c) David, Master of Northesk, Lord Rose-hill, 1719

The first military body, under Government control, to adopt tartan as a part of their uniform was not, as might have been expected, a Highland regiment, but a Lowland one. The Royal Company of Archers in 1713 adopted a red tartan

Courtesy: University of St Andrews 69

ILLUSTRATION FROM DEFOE'S *Life of Duncan Campbell*, SECOND EDITION, 1720

'Our young boy, now between six and seven, delighted in wearing a little bonnet and plaid, thinking it looked very manly in his countryman.' 71

THE MACDONALD BOYS (Artist unknown)

It will be seen that the boys are wearing different tartans, all unknown today

Courtesy: The Rt. Hon. the Lord Macdonald, M.B.E., T.D. facing 72

JAMES FRANCIS EDWARD MORAY, eldest son of the 13th Laird of Abercairny By Jeremiah Davison

The tartan worn is not the same as that shown in the picture facing page 62

Courtesy: His Grace the Duke of Atholl 73

COUNTRY GIRL WEARING PLAID From McIan's *Costumes of the Clans*

'Many women wear, especially the meaner sort, plaids . . . which is cast over their heads, and covers their faces on both sides, and would reach almost to the ground.' Sir William Brereton, 1636 74

ILLUSTRATION FROM BURT'S *Letters from the North, c.* 1730

The four Highlanders are shown, except the second from the left, wearing trews. Two are wearing their plaids drawn over their shoulders in the way a modern shawl might be worn 76

LES ECOSSAIS A PARIS OU LA CURIOSITE DES FEMMES By Genty, 1815

'For the most part they wear the petticoat so very short, that in a windy day, going up a hill, or stooping, the indecency of it is plainly discovered.' Captain Burt, 1726

Courtesy: Scottish United Services Museum 77

UNKNOWN LADY By William Mosman

'The plaid is the undress of the ladies and to a genteel woman who adjusts it with a good air, it is a becoming veil.' Captain Burt in his *Letters from the Highlands,* 1726

Courtesy: The Rt. Hon. Sir Alec Douglas-Home, K.T., P.C.   79

BATTLE OF CULLODEN, 1745 By A. Heckel (a)

This picture of the battle scene was probably made from official observation

Courtesy: Scottish National Portrait Gallery   80

DETAIL FROM BATTLE OF CULLODEN (b)

About this time the lower part of the belted plaid is often shown drawn between the legs. The supporters of the MacPherson coat of arms are dressed the same. Alexander Nisbett in 1722 describes it 'their shirts tied between them'

Courtesy: Scottish National Portrait Gallery   81

SIR STUART THREIPLAND OF FINGASK By William Delacour

Sir Stuart is seen to be wearing his plaid after the fashion of the soldiers at Culloden. A portrait of Alexander Monro, the piper to Prince Charles Edward, shows the kilt also drawn between the legs

Courtesy: Mr and Mrs Mark S. Murray Threipland   83

LORD OGILVY By Allan Ramsay

David, Lord Ogilvy, commanded Ogilvy's Horse in the Jacobite army, 1745. He was attainted and subsequently pardoned on account of his youth

Courtesy: The Rt. Hon. the Earl of Airlie, K.T., G.C.V.O., M.C.   84

PRINCE CHARLES EDWARD

He does not seem to have worn the kilt before the battle of Culloden, but he is often depicted wearing a plaid, the tartans differing greatly. He did wear the kilt when he was hiding in the Highlands

Courtesy: The Rt. Hon. the Earl of Ancaster   86

REBELLION REWARDED, 1746

Some of the figures are wearing belted plaids, some tartan plaids over ordinary dress. It will be noted that those who wear the belted plaid have the lower part pulled between the legs. This method of wearing the costume is often shown in pictures of this period

Courtesy: Scottish National Portrait Gallery   87

THE BELTED PLAID From McIan's *Costumes of the Clans*

The belted plaid was the tartan plaid as an outer garment covering the whole body and gathered at the waist to form a full skirt reaching to the knees   88

DETAILS OF HIGHLAND TROOPS AT MAINZ, 1743

Left: The top part of the belted plaid is being thrown over the left shoulder

Right: The belted plaid is worn over both shoulders as a protection from the rain

Courtesy: Scottish United Services Museum   89

SIR ROBERT DALRYMPLE OF CASTLETON (Artist unknown)

Tartan was worn by Lowland Whig families as well as by Highland Jacobite families, as witness the portrait of the Laird of North Berwick's son, Sir Robert Dalrymple, who was married in the year of the Union

Courtesy: Major Sir Hew Hamilton-Dalrymple, Bt.   facing 90

BLACK WATCH From *The Cloathing Book* drawn up by the War Office, 1742

The first Highland regiment to wear tartan was the famous Black Watch (42nd), raised in 1729. It was called 'Black Watch' after its dark tartan   91

THE HIGHLAND WEDDING By Jacob de Witt (*fl.* 1684–1686)

Several of the men are wearing tartan trews. The plaid is being worn by some of the men and women

Courtesy: Sir John Clerk, Bt.   93

A LOWLAND WEDDING By Jacob de Witt (*fl.* 1684–1686)

The costume is very similar to that shown in 'The Highland Wedding' although no men are shown wearing tartan trews. Several of the men and women are wearing plaids

Courtesy: The Rt. Hon. the Earl of Ancaster   94

HIGHLAND CHIEFS From James Logan's *The Scottish Gael*, 1831

This beautiful hand-painted picture formed the frontispiece of *The Scottish Gael* by James Logan, 1831. It shows the plaid and kilt as separate garments   97

TWO SCOTTISH ROVERS UNDERGOING THEIR VIGIL

The old dress has come back to its earliest use—a dress for those who roam the wild open moors and the steep rugged mountains

Courtesy: John Annandale   99

COLONEL ALASDAIR MACDONELL OF GLENGARRY (1771–1828)
By Sir Henry Raeburn

> He lived outside the period dealt with in this book but the picture illustrates the attempt of some of the chieftains to revive the costume. It certainly makes a handsome figure
>
> *Courtesy: The National Galleries of Scotland*   facing 100

LORD GLENORCHY By C. Jervis, *c.* 1708

> The tartans worn are unknown today
>
> *Courtesy: The Rt. Hon. Armorer Countess of Breadalbane*   105

O, THE ROAST BEEF OF OLD ENGLAND Part of Hogarth's *Gate of Calais*
Engraved by C. Mostey, 1749

> It shows a full length figure of a Scotsman wearing a tartan jacket and trews. He wears a bonnet with the Jacobite white cockade
>
> *Courtesy: Trustees of the British Museum*   111

Prologue

'I have beene at houses like castles for building; the master of the house his beaver being his blue bonnet, one that will weare no other shirts but of the flaxe that growes on his owne ground, and of his wives, daughters or servants spinning; that hath his stockings, hose, and jirkin of the wooll of his owne sheepes backes; that never (by his pride of apparell) caused mercer, draper, silkeman, embroyderer, or haberdasher to break and turne bankcrupt and yet this plaine home-spunne fellow keepes and maintaines thirty, forty, fifty servants, or perhaps more, every day relieving three or foure score poore people at his gate: and besides all this, can give noble entertainment for foure or five days together to five or sixe Earles and Lords, besides Knights, Gentlemen, and their followers, if they be three or foure hundred men and horse of them; where they shall not onely feede but feast, and not feast but blanket. This is a man that desires to know nothing so much, as his duty to God and his King, whose greatest cares are to practise the workes of piety, charity, and hospitality: he never studies the consuming art of fashionless fashions; he never tries his strength to beare foure or five hundred acres on his back at once, his legs are always at liberty, not being fettered with golden garters, and manacled with artificial roses, whose weight (sometime) is the reliques of some decayed lordship. Many of these worthy housekeepers there are in Scotland, amongst some of whom I was entertained.'

The Pennylesse Pilgrimage, by John Taylor, 1618

Foreword

BY SIR IAIN MONCREIFFE
OF THAT ILK, BT.

WE ARE all indebted to Mr Grange for the years of research which he has devoted to this interesting and certainly controversial study of our Scottish national cloth and costume.

His book is of special interest in that it emphasises that tartan — as opposed to the belted plaid or later kilt — was in use in the lowlands as well as in the highlands from a much earlier period than is realised. Tartan, therefore, should be considered a proper symbol of the Scottish way of life, despite the modern fashion of asserting it to be purely highland.

Moreover the distinction between Celtic Highlands and Teutonic Lowlands was never quite so clear-cut as historical generalization has perhaps necessarily led many people to believe. For instance, while MacLeod of MacLeod was of Norwegian origin and the great MacShimi belonged to the Norman or Frankish Fraser family which had also broad lands in lowland Buchan, the Laird of Wemyss in lowland Fife belonged to the premier Gaelic clan — Macduff — and also held lands in the highlands: so that there is a very fine mid-eighteenth century portrait by Allan Ramsay of the Earl of Wemyss clad in tartan.

The Royal Company of Archers, a body which included highland chiefs and lowland lairds alike and which had its headquarters in Edinburgh, adopted a red tartan sett for their uniform as early as 1713. The future King George III was painted in this same tartan uniform as a boy in 1746. Again, tartan was worn by lowland *Whig* families as well as by highland *Jacobite* families — as witness the portrait of the Laird of North Berwick's son, Sir Robert Dalrymple, who was married in the year of the Union.

Also, there is little doubt that when *family* tartans became fashionable, some of the Border and other lowland setts were designed quite as early as many of the best-known highland setts. A list of tartans compiled in 1794 shows 'Bruce sett' as well as 'McDonalds sett': and indeed the famous Nile explorer James Bruce (1730–1794) wore a curious tartan suit which still survives at Broomhall.

Incidentally, those who are interested in the much-disputed question about the antiquity of family or clan tartans should perhaps consider the history of family, estate and regimental tweeds over the past century. A Ramsay who had served in the Scots Guards might wear the Dalhousie tweed or the Invermark tweed or the Scots Guards tweed from time to time, yet have his portrait painted in some other tweed which he had happened to fancy in a tailor's pattern-book when ordering a new suit. The whole question would be finally settled if anybody were able to trace the famous letter said to have been written in 1618 by Sir Robert Gordon of Gordonstoun, and which Mr Grange quotes. It was certainly the sort of letter that Gordonstoun would have written, and in his style, but where is it?

May, 1966   IAIN MONCREIFFE OF THAT ILK
                                                        ALBANY HERALD

Publisher's Note

AN EXTENSIVE search has been made of libraries, galleries and private collections by the Author and the Publishers to try to find paintings hitherto unpublished showing tartan being worn as a part — however small — of the clothes of the sitter. If any reader knows of a portrait painted before 1745, which has never been reproduced before, depicting tartan in any form, we would be grateful if details could be sent to us so that the illustration may be considered for inclusion in future printings of this work.

We would like to make it clear to readers that we have not attempted to publish in this book all the known pictures painted before 1745 showing tartan and which may have been reproduced elsewhere. We are further aware that some which appear in this work are post-1745. Whatever the period, those published have been selected with a view to illustrating, proving or making clear some point in the text, apart from the one or two included because they are fine examples of works of art.

'Highland Dress, the former national costume of the Scottish people, now seen only on ceremonial occasions...'

THE GREAT ENCYCLOPAEDIA OF
UNIVERSAL KNOWLEDGE

CHAPTER ONE

Early Times

WHEN THIS short history of the Scottish dress was first started, it was intended to show only the development of the modern kilt from the earliest times. As the numerous references were collected together over a period of many years and arranged in chronological order, other interesting — and rather startling — facts were brought to light.

Like so many National costumes, the Scottish dress originated from something primitive and easy to make. As time progressed, its usage — being simple — was restricted to those of very limited means and naturally it was in the Highlands that the poorest people were mostly to be found. In that area, it was worn to a far greater degree than elsewhere, and that may account for its being known as the Highland dress. But it was never restricted to that area, nor was it universal there. (A piper of the Argyll militia of 1746 preferred trews to the kilt.) In its form as a belted plaid — that is when a large plaid formed not only the kilt but the plaid as well and was often the only garment worn — it was found amongst the poorest of all districts. There is evidence of this as late as 1678. Incidentally, 'plaid' means 'blanket' in Gaelic, and this accounts for the plaid being often called a blanket.

Until the eighteenth century, when it became a symbol of patriotism, the plaid was never worn generally by the upper classes — Highland or Lowland. It was the simple dress of the poor man. The rich man wore it for hunting, no matter from what district he came, because it was ideal for that purpose; farmers wore it often as a convenient dress for their occupation but it remained generally a dress for the masses who, since its wearing bore no rules or restrictions, modified and altered it to suit their own needs. Thus we find it in many forms but the one distinctive feature in all its forms was the inclusion of tartan. It is that which really makes it Scottish.

3

It seems that tartan — and the tartan plaid — originated in the Lowland districts and its popularity spread to the Highlands. The kilt itself, as separate from the plaid, appears to be only a recent innovation although there are suggestions that it might have been worn much earlier. Tartan trews were popular throughout Scotland.

In 1746 an Act was passed prohibiting the wearing of tartan in any form in Scotland by men and boys. That this Act was not fully obeyed becomes obvious by the many references to tartan worn during the period it was in force and by the number of pictures painted at that time. This is interesting as the Act is so often blamed for the complete break in the history of clan tartans and for the lack of real information on this subject. Many books are published today giving what purport to be authentic *clan* tartans. They are based largely on the prolific writings of early Victorians who concocted vast collections from the flimsiest of evidence — pieces of old material *said* to have been worn by certain ancestors, opinions of elderly people and often from sheer imagination. Certain designs were never reserved for special clans and the wearer always exercised his choice and ingenuity in the matter of what tartan he would like to sport. But there is certainly evidence from about 1600 onwards of a growing desire by the more powerful chiefs to have their men dressed in clothes of a similar pattern.

When tartans were first made in large numbers — generally for export — at the end of the eighteenth century, they were usually referred to by numbers. It is not suggested that they should be sold thus today. Such an idea would be utterly out of sympathy with the whole of Scottish social organization. If anything of the kind had developed the use of the tartan would have long since been killed. The very act of their being given a definite clan or family significance humanized and personalized them. But there are certainly no grounds for sneering at any because they are of recent date. And it must be realized that the lack of a tartan does not debar anyone from adopting one. To do so is but extending the process begun in the early nineteenth century. While the Scottish dress is surrounded by numerous regulations that can only restrict

THE LAIRD OF CLUNY-MACPHERSON (Artist unknown)
This picture shows the plaid being worn with trews, popular with chieftains and
others for winter wear

its adoption to a few people, it has little chance of once again becoming the dress of the ordinary man or woman — and that was certainly what it was. The plaid — the kilt and the belted plaid are only different ways of wearing the plaid — was the dress of the poor man. Those who could afford to copy the fashion of London generally did so. Lord Balmerino at his execution in London (1746) had only an old nightcap to show his loyalty. But he wore it because it was tartan and therefore denoted 'he died a Scottishman'.

A costume that has its origin in the distant past will have passed through many stages before it will have emerged as that which is known today. The modern kilt is no exception.

From the fragments of sculpture, royal seals and a very limited amount of literature we can only conjecture that the dress of those living in Scotland in the earliest times was very similar to those of England or Ireland. It appears to have been a long tunic, generally of one colour. That striped cloth was made is evident from contemporary writers, but this was manufactured widely in Europe as well as in Scotland. Tartan was not unknown in England.

Tacitus says of the Germans (A.D. 93): 'They all wrap themselves in a cloak which is fastened with a clasp . . . leaving the rest of their persons bare', while William of Malmesbury (*c.* 1095–1142) notes that 'the English of that time [arrival of William I] wore short garments reaching to the mid-knee'. Tacitus spent some time in Britain about A.D. 60 and wrote: 'A liking sprang up for our style of dress and the "toga" became fashion- *c.* 206   able', but Dio Cassius wrote of the Caledonians: 'They have no houses 296   but tents, where they live naked.' Eumenius refers to the Picts as 'half *c.* 516–570   naked', and Gildas describes the Scots and Picts as 'covering rather their villainous countenances with hair than the shameful parts of their bodies Died 636   and those next to the shameful parts with clothes'. Isidorus Hispalensis, in his *Liber Etymologicarum*, speaks also of the fact that 'the scottish clothing

6

disfigure them . . . and though they are generally fair of face and of comely bearing, they are much disfigured by their peculiar dress'.

The oldest Scottish tartan preserved is that known as the Falkirk Tartan. *c. 240–250* It dates from the third century and is in two colours, dark brown and a light brown. It was found in Bell's Meadow, north of Callender Park, and was used to protect the mouth of a jar filled with coins.

An early reference to what might be tartan appears in Turgot's *Life* *c. 1050* *of St Margaret*. Turgot was Bishop of St Andrews and lived in the eleventh century. He speaks of 'diversis coloribus vestis', that is, parti-coloured vestments. F. Adam says in his *Clans, Septs and Regiments of the Scottish Highlands* that the robes of the early Scottish Church 'were usually striped or chequered with eight colours'.

It seems that at this early date there was a distinctive Scottish style of dress. Poverty and the lack of communications helped this and in spite of the social influence of the Continent and England, it grew. Repeatedly it was feared that Scotland might lose her identity, and Buchanan in his *History of Scotland* relates how 'Evenus [*c.* 300], in order to reform the manners of the people, which has become corrupted under the late king, recalled the youth to the ancient simplicity in dress, food and common manners'.

'From the beginning of the eleventh century, the history of Scotland is essentially that of the first great English colony; telling how Lothian in the south-east corner, thoroughly Anglican in blood, language and customs, became the predominant partner in a loosely compacted king-dom of Celtic speech and polity. The Anglicans spread northward and westward; their influence spread faster and further; their tongue, their customs and their laws became the national tongue, customs and laws of a heretofore purely Celtic state.' (D. Patrick, LL.D., *Introduction to the Statutes of the Scottish Church*, 1907.) 'The subsequent history of Scotland is the record of that culture's intrusive triumph', wrote C. S. Terry in his *History of Scotland*, 1920.

As that culture spread, so the 'peculiar dress' was confined more and more to those parts where this influence was little felt. But even in the

7

MAP OF SCOTLAND
By John Speed (1552–1629)

This map is interesting as it illustrates well the more primitive form of the dress and is one of the earliest pictures showing tartan

The Yles of Orknay

A Scale of Miles

SUTHERLAND

Caithnes

Strathe Leith

Stranavern

The marble mountaines of Sutherland

Rosse

Ardmanoth

MURAY

BUQUHAN

GARE

Strathbog

Aberdone

New Aberdone

Athole

Dunkell

Broad albayn

Perth

Argile

Lac Lomond

Lennox

Sterling

Steinling

THE GERMANE SEA

Red head

Fife nes

Edynburgh

LOUTHIANE

Twe dale

The Mar

Barwick

Kyle

Anandale

Tivedale

Galloway

PART OF ENGLAND

Carlisle

A Scotch Woman

A Highland woman

Performed by John Speed, and are to be Sold by Thomas Bassett in Fleet street, and Ric Chiswell in St Pauls Church yard.

Lothians itself, it was never completely lost. Here it was modified to conform more nearly to the standards demanded by this culture.

1139–1173   From an old guide to Compostella we read: 'The Navarrese wear dark clothes, short to the knees only, in the manner of the Scots. . . . They wear woollen mantles of dark colour, hanging to the elbows, fringed like a cape.'

1138   Ethelredus of Rievallis reports Walter Espec, a Baron from Yorkshire

FALKIRK TARTAN (*a*)

During levelling operations in Bell's Meadow, north of Callender Park, a workman struck a jar which cracked. Its mouth was filled with this piece of cloth and the jar contained coins dating from 83 B.C. to A.D. 230. There were more than 1,925 in number

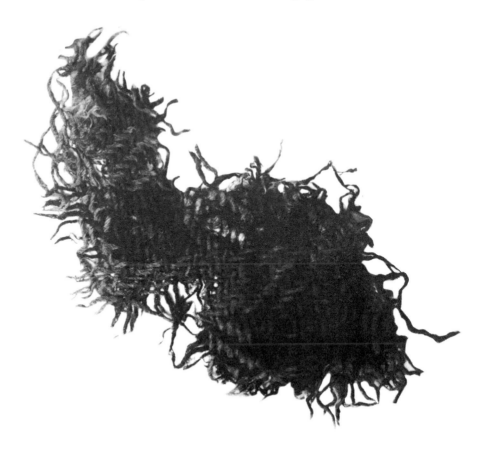

FALKIRK TARTAN (*b*)

'The Falkirk twill is certainly the earliest herringbone recorded for Scotland, and the earliest tartan, too, if we may claim it as such on the strength of the stripes and checks . . . a poor man's plaid with two colours only, dark and light brown.' *Two Textiles from the National Museum, Edinburgh*, by Mrs G. M. Crowfoot

at the Battle of the Standard, as saying that the men of Galloway had 'half-naked buttocks' and nothing but a calf-skin as a shield to protect 'their naked hide'. Ralph de Diceto in *Imagines Historiarum* wrote: '. . . an 1173 endless host of Galwegians, men agile, unclothed, remarkable for much boldness, arming their left side with knives.'

These last two descriptions at least show that the dress of the Scot was cruder than that of the English, and the first gives a hint that it might have been in the form of a short tunic.

c. 1175   Jocelin of Brakeland wrote the following in his *Chronicle*: 'I, however, pretended to be Scotch, and putting on the garb of a Scotchman and taking the gesture of one, walked along, and when anyone mocked at me, I would brandish my staff in the manner of that weapon they call gaveloc [cudgel] uttering comminatory words after the way of the Scotch.' This obviously refers to a costume more advanced. Jocelin would hardly have sallied forth dressed after the fashion of the men of Galloway. But Galloway was far from the influence of Edinburgh, and it was most probably the dress of the latter that he adopted: something more 'cultured' but still bearing its own distinctive style.

XIII Cent.   The General Statutes of the Scottish Church state: 'We further ordain that rectors and vicars of churches . . . shall be becomingly clothed. . . . Let them not wear red or green or striped clothes nor clothes con-

1256   spicuous for too great shortness.' The Chartularies of Aberdeen ordered the ecclesiastics 'to be suitably apparelled, avoiding red, green and striped clothing, and their garments shall not be shorter than the middle of the leg'. This is the first reference to a striped garment reaching to the knees. The Synodal Statutes of St Andrews also mention length: 'We further decree that no priest celebrate in a tunic so short that it does not reach beyond the knee.'

That the standard of clothing varied enormously in Scotland is obvious from the next two references. John Major, in his *History of Greater Britain*, reports Edward II as saying: 'Those among them [Scots army at Ban-

1314   nockburn] that are of more civility have no other shirts than what are made from deers' hides, and the cloaks of their wild men are not other-wise. . . .' This was written in 1521 but Bartholomaeus de Glanvilla in

1360   *De Proprietatibus Rerum* gives the reason — the culture of the Lothians: 'The londe Scotia hathe the name of Scottes that dwelle. The men are lyght of harte, fiers and couragious on theyr enemys . . . and though the men bene seemly ynough of figure and of shape, and fayre of face gener-ally by kind, yet theyr owne scottyshe clothynge dysfygure them full moche. . . . And, bycause of medlyng with englishe men, many of them have changed the olde maners of scottes in to better maners for the more

12

HIGHLAND GRAVE SLAB
'The armour of the knightly effigies found in the West Highlands is a most puzzling affair. One thing I have not found at any place which I have visited—what we now term the Highland Dress.'
James Drummond in *The Sculptured Monuments in Iona and the West Highlands*

FIFTEENTH-CENTURY CORBEL IN THE ABBEY KIRK,
PAISLEY

This corbel depicts a young man wearing a short, kilted tunic, very
much like a modern kilt

parte, but the wylde scottes and Iryshe accounte greate worshyppe to folowe theyr fore fathers in clothynge, in tonge, and in lyvynge, and in other maner doynge.'

1369   The Royal Crest as given in the *Armorial de Gelre* shows, amongst other things, bag-pipes covered in tartan cloth.

14

Bartholomaeus has mentioned the cleavage that had begun between the 'civilized' and 'wild' parts of Scotland. James I did his best to 'civilize' the whole. 'Let God but grant me life,' he said, upon becoming King in 1424, after eighteen years' imprisonment in England, 'and there shall not be a spot in my kingdom where the key doth not keep the castle and the furze-bush keep the cow, though I myself live the life of a dog in bringing it to pass.' James did his best, and the 'culture' of the Lothians spread. Its influence was strong in all the Lowland districts, and it is here that the greatest changes in the dress took place. The more educated people began to look on those living away from this 'culture' as 'wylde' or 'old fashioned'. But by a sumptuary law of Parliament, they compelled the lower classes to retain in some form the old dress even in the Lowlands. 'Na yeman na comonner to landwarts wer hewyt [striped] clathes siddar [lower] na the knee.'   1429

The old chronicler, 'Blind Harry', did not think it unusual to describe Sir William Wallace as wearing an 'Ersche mantill', and even added, 'it war the kynd to wer'. Ersche means Gaelic. And Royalty certainly did not despise tartan. John, Bishop of Glasgow, treasurer to James III, wrote: 1471 'Ane elne and ane halve of blue Tartane to lyne his gowne of cloth of gold. . . . Four elne and ane halve of Tartane for a sparwort aboun his credill. . . . Halve ane elne of doble Tartane to lyne ridin collars to her lade the Quene.' An ell was 37 inches.   *c.* 1470

So far, references to tartan have been confined to the 'more civilized' and the 'wild Scots' appear to have clung to their 'deers' hides'. That   *c.* 1500 may account for Dunbar making a distinction:

> He gat my grandsyr Gog Magog,
> Ay, when he dansit the warld wald shog,
> Five thousand ellis gaed till his frog
> Of Heiland pladdis and mair . . .

Up to this period there are no real descriptions of the Scottish dress. Even the old carvings and monuments do not help us. This puzzled James Drummond, who wrote in his *The Sculptured Monuments in Iona and the West Highlands*: 'The armour of the knightly effigies found in the

15

West Highlands is a most puzzling affair. One thing I have not found at any place which I have visited — what we now term the Highland dress.' There is, however, a small figure in the Abbey Kirk, Paisley, which depicts a young man wearing a short, kilted tunic, very much like a modern kilt.

The answer could lie in the fact that those who could afford monuments could afford 'more civilized' clothes. The dress was usually confined to the poor, but even the descriptions of the west Highland mercenaries who fought in Ireland about these times do not mention tartan. They are repeatedly described as wearing clothes similar to those depicted on the monuments. St Leger (1543) describes these soldiers as 'harnessed in mayle and bassinettes' and Edmund Spenser as 'armed in a long shirt of mayle down to the calfe of the leg'.

1503   The bonnet has always formed part of the dress of the Scot. John Young, who rode with the fifteen-year-old Margaret to meet her future husband, James IV, wrote that the latter wore a 'shirt broidered with thread of gold, his bonnet black with a rich balas [ruby] and his sword about him'. The bonnet was not confined to one colour. The Charters of Peebles mention 'a bonat scarlat' (1457), 'a red bonet' (1458), 'blew bonnettis' (1632). The counsellors were repeatedly asked to wear hats and not bonnets.

DOCTOR NATHANIEL SPENS By Sir Henry Raeburn, 1791
Dr Spens is wearing the uniform of the Royal Company of Archers.
See page 68

CHAPTER TWO

The Saffron Tunic
and the
Tartan Plaid

JOHN MAJOR gives our earliest detailed description of the dress worn by the more remote of the people: 'From the middle of the thigh to the foot they have no covering for the leg, clothing themselves with a mantle instead of an upper garment, and a shirt dyed with saffron. They always carry a bow and arrows and a very broad sword, with a small halbert, a large dagger sharpened on one side only, but very sharp, under the belt. In time of war they cover their whole body with a shirt of mail of iron rings and fight in that. The common people of the wild Scots rush into battle having their bodies clothed with a linen garment sewed together in patchwork and daubed with pitch, with a covering of deerskin.'

Here again, there is no mention of tartan and their plaids are still made of deerskin. Later he adds: 'Their legs are frequently naked under the thigh; in winter they carry a mantle for an upper garment.' Their dress was simple and it might have been this that was worn by the people of Galloway at the Battle of the Standard. They would certainly have appeared to a refined Englishman as 'unclothed'.

Pierre de Ronsard writes of the marriage of James V and Princess Madeleine: 'Ces deux grands Reys, l'un en robe francoyse, et l'autre revestu d'une mantle escossoise.' We know that James V wore tartan in the form of a coat and trews from the Accounts of the Lord High Treasurer of Scotland: '$2\frac{1}{4}$ ells of various coloured velvet for one short Highland coat; 3 ells of Highland 'tertane' [tartan?] to be hose; 15 ells of Holland clothe to be long Highland shirts.' (The old Scots terms have been translated into modern English.)

This is the first reference to 'Highland Tartan', and from this we might assume that the use of tartan was now spreading to the Highlands, or that Highland had a different meaning from what it has today. It seems he wore for hunting a tartan coat and tartan trews since hose meant 'a species of pantaloons fitting closely to the limbs and attached to the waist-coat by strings or laces tipped with metal points'. (Dr C. B. Gunn, *Records of the Baron Court of Stitchill*, 1905.) Nothing is said of a plaid but this, we learnt from Ronsard, he probably had.

Compared with the description by John Major — and others written in later years — this is certainly a very civilized form of the costume generally worn at this time in the Highlands.

James V was very fond of hunting not only in the North Highlands but also in the Southern Uplands. Lindsay of Pitscottie tells us how he 'made proclamation to all lords, barons, gentlemen, landward-men, and free-holders, to compear at Edinburgh, with a month's victual, to pass with the king to daunton the thieves of Teviotdale, etc., and also warned all gentlemen that had good dogs to bring them, that he might hunt in the said country; the Earl of Argyll, the Earl of Huntly, the Earl of Atholl, and all the rest of the Highlands did, and brought their hounds with them, to hunt with the king'. Next year he went to hunt in Atholl.

The Highlands and Southern Uplands were looked upon as great hunt-ing areas and the old Scottish dress was ideally suited to this sport, being light and free.

It has never been decided to what extent of the country the name 'Highland' applied. The above mentions the Earl of Huntly as being a Highlander, and in 1385, when Robert II was at Stirling, he was con-sidered to be in the Highlands. That the term covered a far greater area than today is certain. Since the hills were the hunting grounds, there is a strong suggestion that it referred to all hilly country, and it is likely that the word 'highland' was often used to denote 'hunting'. In old docu-ments an 'uplandis man' meant a man who lived in the country as dis-tinguished from one who lived in town. In the Statute (1594), 'for punishment of theft, oppression, the barbarous cruelties, etc., of the clans and surnames inhabiting the Highlands and Isles', after naming the clans and surnames, there is added 'and others inhabiting the shires of Argyll, Bute, Dumbarton, Stirling, Perth, Forfar, Aberdeen, Banf, Elgin, Forres, Nairne, Inverness, Cromarty, etc.'.

The suitability of the dress for hunting was pointed out by John Elder, a priest, in a letter he wrote to King Henry VIII. 'Moreover, wherefore they call us in Scotland Redshanks, and in your Grace's dominion of England rough footed Scots. Please it your Majesty to understand, that we of all people can tolerate, suffer and alway best with cold, for both summer and winter, except when the frost is most vehement, going always bare legged and bare foot, our delight and pleasure is not only in hunting of red deer, wolves, foxes and graies [badgers], whereof we abound and have great plenty, but also in running, leaping, swimming, shooting and throwing of darts: therefore, in so much as we use and delight so to go always, the tender, delicate gentlemen of Scotland call us Redshanks. . . . And although a great sort of us Redshanks go after this manner in our country, yet nevertheless, and please your Grace, when we come to the Court (the King's Grace our great master being alive) waiting on our Lords and masters, who also, for velvet and silks be right well arrayed, we have as good garments as some of our fellows which give attendance in the court every day.'   **1543**

Here it will be seen that the dress in its old form was not considered suitable for 'town wear'. To attend court 'bare legged and bare foot' would shatter that Lothian culture.

The sixteenth century is most prolific in references to tartans, plaids, detailed descriptions of the dress. It is now possible to build up a better picture of its composition and of its general popularity throughout Scotland.

From the *Burgh Court Book of Elgin*, we find 'and plaid of ten ells price   **1543** 20s', 'touching the claim of one tartan plaid clamed by Andrew Bruce   **1544** from Janet Leslie . . .'. Three years later: 'Murrell Gowre was decerned   **1547** to pay Sir William Sutherland, person of May, 4s. for one plaid' and next year 'Sanders Duff was decerned to deliver a plaid to John Baxstair as   **1548** good as when he got it.' In December of the following year 'Master Slaitter was decerned to deliver one tartain plaid to William Adam'.   **1549**

Meanwhile, the Provincial Council held by the Prelates and Clergy at   **1549** Edinburgh was doing its best to quieten the dress of its members: 'The

TULLOCH OF DUNBENNAN, THE JACOBITE
The sitter wears a tartan coat, a plaid draped over his left shoulder and a dark
bonnet

FRANCIS CHARTERIS, 7TH EARL OF WEMYSS By Allan Ramsay
The Laird of Wemyss lived in Lowland Fife. He held some lands in the Highlands. The picture was painted in 1745

clergy wear only round birettas and shall always take off their caps in churches, especially in choirs and in time of divine service and not dress, as for example, in top-boots and double-breasted or oddly-cut coats, or of forbidden colours, as yellow, green and such kinds of parti-colour.'

1549   Monsieur Jean de Beauque, when describing the Scottish army at the siege of Haddington, says: 'Several wild Scots followed them [the Scottish Army] and they were naked except their stained shirts, and a certain light covering made of various colours; carrying large bows and similar swords and bucklers to the others.'

1552   About this time it was not usual to let these 'wild Scots' go abroad in their 'stained shirt'. An Act of Privy Council was passed for the levy of two regiments of Highlanders for service in France. The Earl of Huntly was directed to see that the men were 'substantiouslie accompturit with jack and plait, steillbonett, sword, bucklair, new hoiss and new doublett of canvouse at the lest, and slevis of plait or spenttis, and ane speir of sax elne lang or thair'by'.

In the more primitive districts, the dress was still in the form of a long tunic repeatedly called a shirt. It appears formerly to have been dyed a saffron colour, but the plaid, or rug of skins, is slowly being replaced by
1562   tartan material. There is a contemporary French woodcut called 'La Sauvage d'Escosse', showing a woman draped in a large cloak of sheep-skins and a chief wearing a quaintly patterned mantle with fringes.

1557   Pierre de Brantôme tells us that Mary, Queen of Scots, insisted more than once on appearing at the French Court 'habillée à la sauvage (comme je l'ay veue) et à la barbaresque mode des sauvages de son pays'. She must have caused a sensation if she looked like the woman in the wood-cut!

1566   It is now generally accepted that this picture is fanciful, but is it really so when we read from the accounts of the celebrations at the baptism of King James VI at Stirling that from twenty-eight goat skins 'was maid four hieland wyld mens cleithings from heid to fute'?

From the Records of Inverness, we get many short references to plaids
1561   and tartans, some of them the first to give actual colours: 'Gilbert Gollan

24

SIR ARCHIBALD BURNETT OF CARLOPS By Richard Wait

He was admitted to the Royal Company of Archers in 1708 and
wears a red tartan

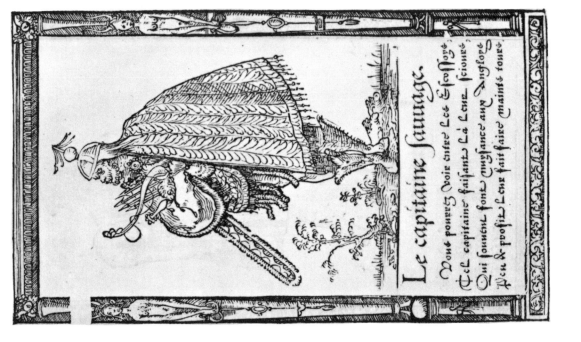

SCOTS IN PARIS,
1562

These pictures are from
a French book called
*Receuil de la Diversité
des Habits* published in
Paris in 1562

1561 is decernit . . . to pay to Arche Anderson or Hendre Kar eldar his factour . . . an gude sufficient plad of V double elnis.' John Cuthbert fails to pay to John Coupland 'ane tartane blew and greyne in compleit payment'.

1563 'Jane Chapman decernit to content and pay to William McFaill, son to Andro MakFaill, alias Textor, ane pair of new schort hois or ellis ane pair

1566 Heland trewis.' Fynla McConylleir 'to pay to Johne Bernis within the town of Pertht the sum of viij gude and sufficient pladdis, fyve dowbill

1566 elne in ilke [each] plad'. Dunsleye is sued for payment for 'an tartan blak and quheit [white] . . . and ane quheit pled quhilk he gaif ane tartan for'.

1567 John Reid, younger son to Sir John Reid, is ordered to pay to David
1567 Johnson of Perth xljs. for three elns and a half of tartan cloth and a blue
1568 bonnet. Bredach Uykermit damages 'ane tartan' worth five marks. Andrew McRobe VcWannycht★ is brought to court for 'drawin sowrd and dingyne at him [Willie Cuthbert] and cutting of his tartan pled'.

1569 Johne Morison claims as son and heir of Donald Morison 'ane blew bonnat, ane grey coit [coat], ane tartan of blak and quheit, ane pair of Heland hois', which has been withheld from him. John Bur travels to

1573 Perth from Inverness and Charles MacGregor steals from his pack 16½ double ells of plaiding and 'ane coit of tartan price xxxs'.

These short excerpts give a glimpse of the many forms in which tartan and the so-called Highland dress was worn in the Lowlands. An old Low-

1568 land poem called 'Sym and his Bruder' mentions 'Twa tabartis of the Tartane'.

Although tartan is certainly popular amongst the more humble of the

1573 Lowland folk and has penetrated into the Highlands, the 'wild Scot' still appears to cling to his saffron shirt, for Lindsay of Pitscottie says: 'They be clothed in one mantle, with one shirt saffroned after the Irish manner, going barelegged to the knee.'

1575 In the Acts and Proceedings of the General Assembly of the Kirk of Scotland, the following ordinance is recorded at the Tolbooth in Edin-

★ 'Son of the son is mac mhic (Mc Vc). Thus John, son of Donald, son of Alan is Iain mac Dhomnuill mhic Ailein (Ian McConnell VcAllan, as a scribe might corrupt it.)'—Sir Iain Moncreiffe of that Ilk, Bt.

26

burgh: 'We think . . . unseemly . . . all using of plaids in the Kirk by Readers and Ministers,' and Aberdeen issued orders to prevent the wearing of plaids by 'burgesses' and 'deakins' of craft 'from the feast of Saint Martin next to come in any time there-after within the burgh'. **1576**

With such orders and opinions it is easy to see why tartan had difficulty in surviving in the towns. Repeatedly it was made quite clear that all good citizens should dress in more sombre clothing. But the unpopularity of this is also quite clear by the repetition of these sumptuary laws during the next century or so. It must also have been most annoying to the city fathers and clergy that Royalty did not back them up for the inventories of the Royal Wardrobe and Jewels of Queen Mary have these entries: 'Ane blue hieland mantill' and 'ane quhite hieland mantill'. **1578**

Bishop Lesley gives an excellent description of the older form of the dress: 'Their clothing was made for use (being chiefly suited for war) and not for ornament. All, both nobles and common people, wore mantles of one sort (except that the nobles preferred those of several colours). These were long and flowing, but capable of being neatly gathered up at pleasure into folds. I am inclined to believe that they were the same as those to which the ancients gave the name of brachae. Wrapped up in these for their only covering, they would sleep comfortably. They had also shaggy rugs, such as the Irish use at the present day, some fitted for a journey, others to be placed on a bed. The rest of their garments consisted of a short woollen jacket, with sleeves open below for the convenience of throwing darts, and a covering for the thighs of the simplest kind, more for decency than for show or defence against cold. They made also of linen very large shirts, with numerous folds and wide sleeves, which flowed abroad loosely to their knees. These, the rich coloured with saffron and others smeared with some grease to preserve them longer clean among the toils and exercises of a camp, which they held it of the highest consequence to practise continually. In the manufacture of these, ornament and a certain attention to taste were not altogether neglected, and they joined the different parts of their shirts very neatly with silk thread, chiefly of a red or green colour.' **1578**

27

FLORA MACDONALD (1722–1790) By Allan Ramsay
She helped Prince Charles Edward to escape to Skye. She was arrested and imprisoned
but was later released

In another part, he refers to the Gaelic as the old Scottish language, and says they 'have hitherto kept the institutions of their elders so constantly, that not only more than two thousand years they have kept the tongue hale and uncorrupt, but likewise the manner of clothing and living, that old form they unchanged absolutely have kept. In this such a reverend fear and dread they have lest they offend in things of honesty, that if their Princes, or of their nobility, visit the King's Court, they array themselves of a courtly manner, elegantly; when they return to their country, casting off courtly decore, in all haste, they clothe themselves of their country manner.'

Here again, it is seen that the older and more crude form of the Scottish dress is considered as suitable only for country wear. This style of dress was still very primitive but it was improving. No longer was it mainly a long tunic. The tartan plaid was being adopted by the wealthier of them; the rug — probably of sheep or goat skin — was still used, but jackets of sorts had been introduced. Slowly the modern form of Highland dress was taking shape. It was admirable for fording streams and walking through wet heather, but certainly not suitable for town wear, especially when one remembers the steep stairs and sloping wynds of Edinburgh! This seems to have been the type of dress that James V bought in 1538 but he added trews!

Allan Ramsay of Inverness claimed twenty bolls of salt sold for twenty   1579
white plaids. James Farquharson confesses to selling unlawfully twenty-five plaids to an Edinburgh man and John Dunbar of Inverness also is hauled over the coals for selling plaids unlawfully.

From George Buchanan we find that the use of tartan was growing   1581
very popular now in the Western Isles. It made excellent camouflage: 'They delight in variegated garments, especially stripes, and their favourite colours are purple and blue. Their ancestors wore plaids of many colours [there is no evidence of this] and numbers still retain this custom, but the majority now in their dress prefer a dark brown, imitating nearly the leaves of the heather, that when lying upon the heath in the day, they may not be discovered by the appearance of their clothes; in these

5

wrapped rather than covered, they brave the severest storms in the open air, and sometimes lay themselves down to sleep even in the midst of snow.'

1583　　'Thomas Purs, wobstar in Elgin, becom actit to work and wyff to Patrick Rattray tuentie hand plaidis.'

1583　　The descriptions of the more primitive form of dress are still very confusing: they tend to contradict one another. From Nicolay d'Arfeville we understand that the saffron tunic is still the main garment: 'Those who inhabit Scotland to the South of the Grampian Mountains are tolerably civilized and orderly, and speak the English language; but those who inhabit the North are more rude, homely and unruly, and for this reason are called "Wild". They wear like the Irish a large and full shirt, coloured with saffron, and over this a garment hanging to the knee, of coarse wool, after the fashion of a cassock. They go barehead, and let their hair grow very long, and wear neither hose nor shoes, except some who have boots made in an old-fashioned way, which come as high as their knees.'

To many of the visitors to Scotland 'those who inhabit the North' appear unruly and wild. Certainly their attire may have been primitive but it is quite incorrect to suppose that there was no discipline in the Highlands and that the Law of the country did not extend to that area. This common assumption — even by modern writers — is quite refuted by the records of Highland districts. It is surprising to find that the justice administered was very similar to that found in any Lowland town. The Inveraray Castle manuscripts confirm this.

1587　　There is a reference in the Charter of the lands of Norraboll in Islay in favour of Hector Maclean, in which it states that the feu duty was payable in the form of sixty ells of cloth of white, black and green colours. The recognized Hunting Tartan of the Macleans today contains the colours white, black and green, but the arrangement of them is taken from 'Vestiarium Scoticum', a list of tartans produced in 1842 by the Stuart brothers, which is generally accepted as pure imagination on their part, and whose authors knew of this Charter. Later, the lands were granted to Rory MacKenzie of Coigeach and the colours were changed to white,

HIGH BOOTS

'They go barehead, and let their hair grow very long, and wear neither hose nor shoes, except some who have boots made in an old-fashioned way, which come as high as their knees.' Nicolay d'Arfeville, 1583

M CORY.

black and grey. The Mackenzie tartan is quite different, but then the Stuart brothers did not know of the second charter. It is repeatedly claimed that here is the first reference to clan tartan: it is difficult to believe Hector Maclean would have consented to give his 'colours' to the Crown to dispose of as it wished.

What it does show is that the local people were now weaving coloured cloth and its use was becoming more general in these parts in place of the usual saffron. 'The collection of these cumbrous produce rents must have imposed a heavy burden on the Chamberlain and his assistants. . . . In 1541, however, there is a note attached to the Morven rental to the effect that "all the martis, cheis and mele are sauld for silver to the tennants of the ground, as Kintyir is", from which we infer that, by this date, the Crown Chamberlain had found means to commute the produce rents into money on the spot' — Andrew McKerral, 'The Tacksman and his Holding,' *Scottish Historical Review*, April, 1947.

From the Register of St Andrews Kirk Session, we read that a certain 1589 indiscreet Mr Andrew Alanis gave Margret Scott 'ane pair of plaidis and mony tymes silver and last xxxs' as a bribe.

ALEXANDER ROBERTSON OF BROWNSBANK, PRENDERGUEST, AND
GUNSGREEN IN THE COUNTY OF BERWICK (1748–1804) By William Mosman

This portrait was painted when he was six years old in 1754, during the
proscription of tartan

The saffron shirt is the common wear among the Highlands, but there 1591 appears a reference in MS *History of the Gordons* which seems to point to a special yellow coat that the chiefs wore in fights: 'In the meanetime, one creeps out under the shelter of some old ruins, and levels with his piece at one of the Chanchattan cloathed in a yellow warr coat (which, amongst them, is the badge of the Chieftanes or heads of Clans).'

A body of auxiliaries from Scotland helped Red Hugh O'Donnell, 1594 Lord of Tirconall, in Ulster against Queen Elizabeth. These warriors were described by Peregrine O'Clery as wearing 'a mottled garment with numerous colours hanging in folds to the calf of the leg, with a girdle round the loins over the garment'.

'Andro Smith [of Moray] was indicted for receiving . . . certane littit 1595 worsettis of the quhilk worsettis thow maid ane tartan plaid to they wife,' and John Campbell of Auchinryre has to pay yearly £10 Scots, 1596 one gallon aquavite [whisky], one very good coloured cloak and one common 'fyne hewed brahane [tartan plaid]'.

Moryson in his *Itinerary* says: 'The inferior sort of citizen's wives, and 1598 the women of the country, did wear cloaks made of a coarse stuff, of two or three colours, in checker work, vulgarly called Ploddan.' From the accounts of David Wedderburne of Dundee, we learn that Lady Westhall 1598 bought his wife's plaid.

This is the period when the dress of the remoter districts changed quickly. The warmer tartan plaid supersedes the saffron tunic. Up to now, the costume has changed little in those districts whose poor communications cut them off from the 'culture of the Lothians', and the dictates of the city fathers have had little influence on them.

Some influence it did have in that those people were quite conscious that their clothes were hardly suitable for town wear. As communications improved, so did their dress, and especially amongst their nobility, who mostly wore the fashions of the more cultured districts. That the towns were fast forsaking the plaid is only true with regard to the wealthy: to the very poor it was still their only outer garment, and in some areas of the so-called Lowland districts it formed their *only* clothing.

1600   Glasgow was not slow in trying to remove every trace; to meet 'his Majestie' it is ordained that the freemen shall not wear their 'blew bonnettis'.

1603   Thomas Dalgleis, burgess of Inverness, is ordered to pay to Ferquhar MackAllister of 'Dunzcan croy, ane gray plaid, a tartan, of fiv elnis doubil'. So often are these plaids stated to be five ell double. A Scots ell was 37 inches (in Dunkeld the old Scots ell is portrayed on the corner of a house in the Square) and so these plaids were very commodious garments,

1603
1606   sufficient to cover quite loosely the whole body. George Fruid is accused of buying 'white plaids' from unfree men in the 'Chanonrie of Ross'. Murdo Poulson of Inverness is ordered to restore a white plaid stolen from John MacAndrew.

1607   Camden, in his *Britannia*, gives a neat little picture of the 'wild Scot': 'They are clothed after the Irish fashion, in striped mantles, with their hair thick and long. In war they wear an iron head-piece and a coat of mail woven with iron rings; and they use bows and barbed arrows and broad swords.'

Repeatedly mention is made of white plaids. It appears that these were generally used for blankets: they were certainly more expensive than

1607   tartan ones. The weavers of Inverness were fined for 'taiking mair nor sex penneis for the elne blew and greine tartan weaving and fourtie penneis for ane quheit [white] plaid weaving, four penneis for the elne of

1613   gray and blaik weaving'. Johne McVirrick received £4 for 'ane quheit plaid that was directit be him to James Vinram', both of Inverness. One had to have a licence to sell plaids.

At the end of the sixteenth century, Lady Montgomery, wife of Sir Hugh Montgomery, 'set up and encouraged linen and woollen manufactory [in Ulster], which soon brought down the prices of the breakens [tartans] and narrow cloths of both sorts'.

JAMES, 5TH EARL OF WEMYSS *c.* 1715
In the uniform of the Royal Company of Archers. The tartan was later changed to a green sett. See page 68

CHAPTER THREE

The Belted Plaid
and the
Sombre Broadcloth

ABOUT THE year 1600 we find a considerable change in the dress outside the 'cultured' districts. The old saffron tunic is gradually dropped and in its place comes the large belted plaid, or the plaid with trews. Tartan is the general pattern now, and fashionable coats make their appearance. This form of dress — perhaps adopted from the Lowland plaids of 'five elnes doubil' — was a great advancement on the tunic, and lent itself to many adornments. The belted plaid was the tartan plaid as an outer garment covering the whole body, and gathered at the waist to form a full skirt reaching to the knees. The trews, or tartan trousers, worn with a smaller plaid over the shoulders, were favoured more by the gentry, chiefly because they rode horseback and the belted plaid was still worn far too short!

The highhandedness of the magistrates of Glasgow is exemplified in their dealing of William Watson, who was accused of using 'disdaynfull speichis' and refusing to take off 'his bonet' to the bailie. 1612

Donald Andrew McAine was hanged for stealing from Alexander 1616 Taillour in Coniegavel a grey plaid and from Thomas Fraser in Kilravock a coat and a pair of breeches. The daughter of David Wedderburne of 1616 Dundee buys the plaid of her deceased sister, Janet, for £11.

About this time Richard James (1592–1638) writes of the Highlanders 1617 that 'their garments are a blue frise slasht jerkin and pleidens and truces and blacke and greene and blue bonnets'.

One of the best descriptions of the belted plaid comes from John 1618 Taylor, the Water Poet. His description is of greater interest because he tells how everyone, Highland or Lowland, wore it when hunting in the Highlands: 'There [Braemar] did I find the truly noble and right honourable Lords, John Erskine, Earl of Mar, James Stuart, Earl of Moray, George Gordon, Earl of Enzie, son and heir to the Marquess of Huntley, James Erskine, Earl of Buchan and John, Lord Erskine, son and heir to the

JOHN STUART, 3RD EARL OF BUTE (1713–1792) In the collection
of the Marquess of Bute (probably by William Aikman *c.* 1730)

This form of the dress was favoured by the nobility

Earl of Mar, and their Countesses, with my much honoured and my best assured and approved friend, Sir William Murray, knight, of Abercarny, and hundred of other knights, esquires, and their followers; all and every man in general in one habit. . . . For once in the year, which is the whole month of August, and sometimes part of September, many of the nobility and gentry of the kingdom (for their pleasure) do come into these high-land countries to hunt, where they do conform themselves to the habit of the high-land-men, who, for the most part, speak nothing but Irish; and in former times were those people which were called the Redshankes. Their habite is shoes with but one sole apiece; stockings (which they call short hose) made of a warm stuffe of divers colours, which they call Tartan: as for breeches, many of them, nor their forefathers, never wore any, but a jerkin of the same stuffe that their hose is of, their garters being bands and wreaths of hay or straw, with a plaid about their shoulders, which is a mantle of divers colours, much finer and lighter stuffe than their hose, with blue flat caps on their heads, a handkerchief knit with two knots about their necks: and thus are they attired. . . . As for their attire, any man of what degree soever that comes amongst them, must not disdain to wear it, for if they do, then they will disdain to hunt, or willingly to bring in their dogs: but if men be kind unto them, and be in their habit, then are they conquered with kindness, and the sport will be plentiful. This was the reason I found so many noblemen and gentlemen in those shapes.'

It appears that a desire for uniformity in the colours of the tartan worn   1618
by their men was now growing amongst the large landowners. A letter from Sir Robert Gordon of Gordonstoun to Murray of Pulrossie requests him 'to furl his pennon when the Earl of Sutherland's banner was displayed and to remove the red and white lines from the plaides of his men so as to bring their dress into harmony with that of the other septs'.

Aberdeen issues orders to prevent women from wearing plaids and the   1621
Elgin Kirk Session forbids women holding plaids about their heads during   1624
the sermon. At the meeting of the Synod of Moray at Elgin it is com-   1624
plained that some of the ministers 'haunts to ye prebie with uncomely

habits, such as bonats and plaides; whairfor the Assemblie ordaines them not to haunt ye prebie anymair with uncomely habitts'.

1629 'The said day Abrahame Forfar, being persewit be Alexander Fraser, officiar, for deforcing him in taking ane plaid from him quhilk he had poyndit from the said Abrahame for his dissobedience, being warnit to have cariet corne frome Montquheiche [a mill six miles from Stonehaven] to Urie.'

1631 The towns are tightening up the laws on dress and Edinburgh forbids women to wear plaids over their heads under a penalty of £5 Scots and the forfeiture of the garment.

1633 When Charles I visited Edinburgh, Maitland, in his *History of Edinburgh*, tells that 'at the top (of the Row) was erected a triumphal arch and here he was addressed by a female dressed in the ancient garb, and representing the figure of Caledonia', and yet in the same year the Edinburgh Town Council passed a new act decreeing corporal punishment for those who

1633 disobeyed that of 1631. Aberdeen also had difficulty. This time women 'of gude qualitie', and others, wearing plaids about their heads, shall have them marked with tar and taken away from them.

1636 Sir William Brereton describes these tiresome plaids: 'Many [women] wear, especially the meaner sort, plaids, which is a garment of the same woollen stuff whereof saddle cloths in England are made, which is cast over their heads, and covers their faces on both sides, and would reach almost to the ground, but that they pluck them up and wear them cast under their arms.'

From him we learn how quickly the Highlander was adapting his clothes to the dictates of society: 'Many Highlanders we observed in this town [Edinburgh] in their plaids, many without doublets, and those who have doublets have a kind of loose flap garment hanging loose about their breech, their knees bare; they inure themselves to cold, hardship and will not diswont themselves; proper, personable, well-complexioned men, and able men; the very gentlemen in their blue caps and plaids.' How many of these so-called Highlandmen were just local small lairds or tacksmen?

40

GERMAN WOODCUT, 1631

Although described as Irish, these are really Scottish soldiers, probably of Mackay's Regiment who took
part in the capture of Stettin in 1630

1641   There is a quaint German woodcut of the Scots in Mackay's Regiment in the service of Gustavus Adolphus. Three of the men are in the belted plaid and one is wearing tartan trews, but these are full and baggy above the knees, a most unusual style. Trews were always cut tight to the leg. It is a crude picture, obviously not executed from close observation.

1641   Robert Gordon of Straloch mentions these trews: 'In the sharp winter, the Highland men wear close Trowzes which cover the Thighs, Legs and Feet. . . . Above their shirt they have a single coat, reaching no farther than the Navel. Their uppermost Garment is a loose Cloke of several Ells, striped and partly coloured, which they gird breathwise with a leather Belt, so as it scarce covers the knees. . . . Far the greatest part of the Plaid covers the uppermost parts of the Body. Sometimes it is all folded round the Body about the Region of the Belt, for disengaging and leaving the hands free; and sometimes 'tis wrapped round all that is above the Flank. The Trowzes are for Winter use; at other times they content themselves with short Hose, which scarce reach to the Knees.'

1641   The city council of Glasgow 'ordanit that same Holland cloathe and Scottis linning cloathe, with sume plydes, be sent as a propyne to Maister Web [the Duke of Lennox's servant]'. James Peir, 'borne in Nisbit, besyid Haddingtoun', is convicted of assaulting John Crombie and the magistrates 'ordanes the said James the best plaid, with his pistole and ane pair of blewshankis, to be presentlie apprysit fer paying the officiaris of suche money as is restand to thame, and the superplus to be delyverit to the chirurgiane. Whilk guides wer instantlie delyverit and apprysit, the plaid at aucht pundis, the pistoll at tuantie sevin shilingis and the shankis at saxtein schilingis.'

1642   The 'provost, baillies and counsell' ordain that the bursars within the college of Aberdeen wear a black gown and black hat or black bonnet upon the streets.

1645   Elgin has a bad time with plaids: March 19th —John Chalmer was ordered to restore to Thomas a two handed sword with 'ane halfe fyte' plaid which he has taken out of Thomas' house. Was a 'half' plaid used as a kilt only: that is, not as a belted plaid? May 30th —Margaret Cay was told to redeliver to William Hay one tartan plaid worth £6. June 4th —Elspet Portisfield of Ardcannie was given back her new tartan plaid taken in 'time of troubles'. William Hay in Neither Manbeines got back his grey plaid for which he had to pay Christian Gordon 'ane halfe dollar'.

And Edinburgh is still having bother with the women. This time the officers are told to seize any women they find wearing plaids and to bring them up for punishment. It is no wonder that the plaid was losing its popularity in the towns. It is amazing that such laws did not stop it altogether from being worn. But fortunately repressive laws often have the opposite effect to what is intended! `1648`

Thomas McKenzie of Pluscardin and his tenants are plundered by Highlanders who take, amongst other things: 'ane whyt plaid worth eight pounds with coat and trews and shoes worth four pounds scots . . . and pair of bed plaides worth twentie four pounds . . . ten elnes of tartan at threttie shillings the elne'. It seems from this that white plaids were not always used for blankets since this distinction is so clearly made. `1649`

The *Wardlaw MS* tells us that Charles II had eighty pipers in his army. `1650`

A pathetic picture from the Minister of Kirkhill: 'I set down that which I myself was an eye witness of. On the 7 May at Lovat [near Inverness], Montrose sat upon a little shelty horse without a saddle, but a bundle of rags and straw, and pieces of ropes for stirrups; his feet fastened under the horse's belly, and a bit halter for a bridle. He had on a dark, reddish plaid, and a cap on his head; a muscateer on each side and fellow-prisoners on foot after him. Thus he was conducted through the country.' `1650`

And Elgin still has trouble with the ladies, and orders their plaids to be taken away when they sit on the 'stool of repentance'. The Provost of Glasgow 'maid report of the committees . . . that they had aggried of new with Simon Pichersgill for a uther yeir for fourtie fyve punds sterling, a sute of cloathes to himselfe and a pair of plydes to his wife.' `1651`

Andrew Mihill of Elgin is fined for stealing a pair of white plaids and two years later Thomas Clark profanes the Sabbath by sewing men's plaids together during church time. `1652` `1654`

1656   Richard Franck, who wrote of his experiences as a trooper in Scotland, mentions 'tartans' among the various goods traded at Glasgow. When at Jedburgh, he said, 'Oat-straw was our sheets, and portmantles our pillows. It's true some had cloaks, and 'twas well they had, otherwise they had been constrained to use plads'.

1657   Alexander Hay furnished one feather bed, bolster, two pair of plaids and a covering to the 'garisone of Dumfermling House in Elgin'.

1659   Sir George MacKenzie published a book on heraldry. In it, he refers to the supporter of the arms of the Burnetts of Leys as 'a Highlander in Hunting Garb'. (Incidentally, Sir George Burnett, Lyon King of Arms

44

From MAP OF ABERDEEN, 1661 By James Gordon of Rothiemay
(1615–1686)

Gordon's *Map of Aberdeen* shows a figure of what appears to be a boy
wearing a kilt. He gave a detailed description of the dress in his *History
of Scots Affair*, explaining several ways in which the plaid could be
worn. He does mention one way as 'folded all round the body about
the region of the belt'

in *The Family of Burnett of Leys* (1901), described the figure as 'a man in
Lowland hunting garb'.) The illustration is taken from the Coat of Arms
in plaster at Muchalls in Kincardineshire, which was finished about 1627.

c. 1660   Mr A. E. Haswell Miller, Keeper of the Scottish National Portrait
Gallery, writing in 1947 on 'Chieftain' by Michael Wright says: 'The
date of Wright's portrait must be somewhere about 1660 and it certainly
shows a kind of check pattern, although apparently not symmetrically
squared and repeated as in the modern tartan. It is, of course, not easy to
paint tartan; and it is not impossible that Wright could not face making

7TH EARL OF ARGYLL, Justice-General of Scotland. Died 1638
Although not clear from this reproduction, the figure is wearing tartan
ribbons at the neck and the garters. He is in Spanish uniform, having entered
the service of Philip III of Spain

an accurate copy of the so complicated drapery. The colours are brown, black, with occasional crimson stripes on a cool buff ground, and certainly bear no resemblance whatever to a Breadalbane tartan of today, as, since the picture is supposed to be a Breadalbane one, might be expected.' (*S.M.T. Magazine*, November, 1947.)

1661 Gordon's Map of Aberdeen shows a figure of what appears to be a boy wearing a kilt and he describes it as 'folded all round the body about the region of the belt'. It is very similar to the supporter on the Burnett Arms.

1662 Charles II, on the occasion of his marriage to Catherine of Portugal, decorated himself with tartan ribbons.

c. 1662 A good picture of the Lowland Scot is obtained from John Reay, Fellow of Trinity College, Cambridge: 'We travelled to Dunbar, a town noted for the fight between the English and Scots. The Scots generally (that is, the poorer sort) wear, the men blue bonnets on their heads, and some russet: the women only white linen, which hangs down their backs as if a napkin were pinned about them. When they go abroad, none of them wear hats, but a party coloured blanket, which they call a plod, over their heads and shoulders. . . . The people seem to be very lazy, at least the men, and may be frequently observed to plow in their cloaks. It is the fashion of them to wear cloaks when they go abroad, but especially on Sundays.'

1672 But still plaids were considered not 'quite correct' wear by the aristocracy of the day. The Chief of the MacNaughtons, who had raised a small troop of bowmen for the King, entreated the Earl of Morton, whom he was to meet on the Isle of Wight, to send suitable clothes 'for they cannot muster before your lordship in their plaids and blue caps'.

1673 James McKenzie, who came from Muirallhouse, causes a riot in the Court at Aberdeen by drawing 'a sword and pistoll, whereby the Court immediately dissolved in confusion and disorder. . . . Having gone down the stair of the Tolbooth wanting his plaid . . . he raised a tumult in the Mercat place.'

1678 There are so many references to the dress of the Scots about this date that there is no object in printing them all. Where any gives a new light on the subject, it is then important. In Thomas Kirke's *Account of Scotland*, he describes in detail the similarity between the clothes of the poorer people of the 'Low-land' and those of the 'High-land': 'Their banks and borders of these rivers (especially near their towns) are adorned with hardy amazons, though inverted, their valour being (chiefly) from the waste downwards, which parts they readily expose to all the dangers of a naked rencounter. . . .

'The habit of the people is very different according to the qualities and places they live in, as Low-land or High-land men. The Low-land gentry go well enough habited, but the poorer sort go (almost) naked, only an old cloak, or part of their bed-clothes thrown over them. The High-landers wear slashed doublets, commonly without breeches, only a plad tyed about their wastes, etc., thrown over their shoulders: with short stockings to the gartering place, their knees and part of their thighs being naked: others have breeches and stockings all of a piece of plad ware, close to their thighs. . . . The women are commonly two-handed tools . . . the meaner go barefoot and bare-headed, with two black elf-locks on either side their faces; some of them have scarce any cloaths at all, save part of their bed-cloathes pinn'd about their shoulders and their children have nothing else on them but a little blanket; those women that can purchase plads, need not bestow much upon other cloaths, these cover-sluts being sufficient. Those of the best sort that are very well habited in their modish silks, yet must wear a plad over all for the credit of their country.'

The above is of importance in bearing out the point that the Scottish costume was never confined to the Highlands. The poorest people of both districts dressed much the same. It is in the middle class that we find the greatest difference: the Highlander in his belted plaid and the Lowlander in his English dress and plaid. In the upper class the Highlander wore his English dress with sometimes a plaid and the Lowlander just the English dress. And we here begin to see the growth of national pride and a symbol for this was Tartan — 'for the credit of their country'.

1685   In Dingwall, Mr Gordon has trouble over a white plaid. Katherine nic coil voire was accused of stealing 'ten elns of white plaid' and 'she proffered ye said white plaid to Mr Gordon and his wife'. And 'Mary nin doil uyre [a poor effort to spell the name] deponed she was in certaine knowledge of her stealing . . . ane white plaid from the said Mr Gordon and his wiffe'.

1685–1686   An interesting distinction is made between Highland and Lowland plaids in a list of articles stolen by the Atholl men when they raided Argyllshire: at Kilcattan they took from the wife of John Duncanson, late minister: '1 Lowland playd mantle, etc . . . £12-0-0; 4 pair sprainged playds . . . £46-13-4; a Highland plaid with some oyr cloathes, linen and woolen . . . £6-13-4.' Would the distinction between 'Highland' and 'Lowland' be the difference between a belted plaid of coarse material and a short shoulder plaid of finer cloth and colours such as might be worn in the Lowlands? The 'List of Depradations' goes on to mention that in Islay, Marie Campbell, 'relict of umgle [the late] Ion M'Caris of Donnardrie is robbed, among other things of 'two pair of Truise [trews] . . . £2-0-0; four elnes of plaiden . . . £1-6-8; one small plaid at . . . £6-13-4'. In Campbeltown they take 'one meet cassick [cassock] and 1 pair of breeches worth £8'. So trousers were worn by some!

1688   The belted plaid started as the entire clothing, but now it had become the outer garment only, and was worn with an eye for decoration. Its ample folds allowed ingenuity in the way it was worn. William Sacheverell, Governor of the Isle of Man, writing of the Isle of Mull, shows how becoming this dress was: 'The usual outward habit of both sexes is the pladd; the women's much finer, the colours more lively, and the squares larger than the men's, and put me in mind of the ancient Picts. This serves them for a veil and covers both head and body. The men wear

LORD DUFFUS (1670–1750) By Richard Wait
Thomas Kirk describes such a dress in 1678 'The Highlanders wear slashed doublets, commonly without breeches, only a plad tyed about their wastes, etc., thrown over their shoulders'

50

theirs after another manner, especially when designed for ornament: it is loose and flowing, like the mantles our painters give their heroes. Their thighs are bare, with brawny muscles. Nature has drawn all her stroakes bold and masterly.'

Whilst this does not actually say that the arrangement of the colours of the women's plaids were completely different from the men's, it does seem to convey the idea that a choice of colour and pattern existed. One rather feels that in describing the colouring to this extent the author would have mentioned clan tartans if these had been universal.

It is important to remember that not only were the Highlands repeatedly planted with Lowlanders (Act of Exchequer of 1609; plantation in 1650 by the Marquis of Argyll, etc.,) but the early rentals of any one district show the surnames not to be solely that of the clan said to inhabit that district, but to be as varied as those in any Lowland district. This is in spite of what Nicol Graham wrote of the central Highlands in 1747: 'As this hath been an ancient custom, most of the farmers and cottars are of the name and clan of the proprietor; and, if they are not really so, the proprietor either obliges them to assume it, or they are glad to do so, to procure his protection and favour', and the Statistical Account for Bedrule (Roxburgh): 'For then it was the pride of the laird or master, to have his tennants, retainers, and even domestics of his own surname.' In many documents we find the term 'Native men' applied to certain people. These native men were not nor did they claim to be 'of the blood of the individual whom they acknowledged to be their chief. They appear to have formed the bulk of the population of the Highlands and to have descended from the ancient occupants of the soil; whilst the clan properly so called consisted only of the blood relations of the chief. By degrees, however, the word clan received a wider interpretation, and embraced all who fought under the banner of the chief, among whom, of course, were included all the able-bodied men dwelling on his lands, whether his kinsmen or his native men.' (Footnote in *Collectanea de Rebus Albanicis*, Iona Club, Vol. I, 198.) In the list of killed or wounded in the campaign 1745–6, of Stewart of Appin's men, eighteen different clan names appear.

52

THE BELTED PLAID By Sir David Wilkie

This very fine drawing shows the dress of the poorest Highlander. It consists solely of a plaid forming the complete dress, leaving the legs and an arm bare

1689   Thomas Morer (*A Short Account of Scotland*) gives a good description of the belted plaid. He says they 'are about seven or eight yards long, differing in fineness according to the abilities or fancy of the wearers. They cover the whole body with 'em from the neck to the knees, excepting the right arm, which they mostly keep at liberty. Many of 'em have nothing under these garments besides waistcoats and shirts which descend no longer than the knees, and they go gird 'em about the middle as to give 'em the same length as the linen under 'em and thereby supply the defect of drawers and breeches.' Of the Lowlander, he says: 'their habit is mostly English, saving that the meaner sort of men wear bonnets instead of hats and pladds instead of cloaks: and these pladds the women also use in their ordinary dress when they go abroad, either to market or church. They cover head and body with 'em and are so contrived as to be at once both a scarf and hood. The quality go thus attired, when they would be disguised and is a morning dress good enough when some hasty business calls them forth, or when the weather disheartens 'em to trick themselves better ... This is all that occurs at present concerning the Lowlands as before distinguished. What I add more treats of the Scotch in common. Their ordinary women go barefoot, especially in the summer. Yet the husbands have shoes, and therein seem unkind in letting their wives bear those hardships without partaking themselves. Their children fare no better.'

It will be seen from this and the description by William Sacheverall (1688) that there is little difference between the Highland and Lowland form of dress for women.

1691   In the descriptive poem called 'The Gramied', about the campaign of Viscount Dundee, written by James Phillip of Almerieclose, there are many details given of the colours worn by the various chiefs and their men: Keppoch, a tartan plaid; the inhabitants of the Hebrides, clothed in yellow and blue; Glengarry has three hundred illustrious youths, each of whom a tartan garb covers, woven in triple stripe; M'Martin wore a saffron plaid; Maclean of Duart, a flowing plaid with yellow stripe: Mac-Neill of Barra had many colours woven into his plaid.

54

In 1587, the reference to the feu duty payable to Maclean of Duart in the form of sixty ells of cloth stated that it should be of white, black and green colours. This has often been claimed as the first reference to a definite clan tartan. Then why is a 'flowing plaid with yellow stripe' now being worn by Maclean? But here again is found the growing desire to have one's men wearing the same type of plaid as is shown by those 'three hundred illustrious youths' of Glengarry, 'each of whom a tartan garb covers, woven in triple stripe', although the modern Glengarry tartan contains five different colours.

No definite mention so far has been made of the kilt as it is known today: that is, a short skirt separate from the plaid. Martin Martin in '*A Voyage to St Kilda*' does mention a very primitive form of such a dress: 'Their Habit antiently was of Sheepskins, which has been worn by severall of the Inhabitants now living; the Men at this day wear a short Doublet reaching to the waste, about that a double Plaid of Plad, both ends join'd together with the Bone of a Fulmar; this Plad reaches no further than their Knees, and is above the Haunches girt about with a Belt of Leather.' 1698

Lady Grisell Baillie of Jerviswood spent £85 5s. (Scots) on 'Scots tartan muslin' at Prestonpans. This was probably made into night clothes because later in 1707 she writes 'for Scots muslin for night clothes'. 1697

Captain Slezer, in his *Theatrum Scotiae*, has several illustrations, amongst which are plates of Falkland, Montrose, Dunkeld, Dunblane, Dunnottar, Elgin, Roslin, St Andrews, Ayr, Gordon Castle and Heriots Hospital. He made the drawings for these engravings during an official survey of Scottish towns and it is reasonable to assume he would not misrepresent the dress of the people. All the above plates show figures in tartan plaids or trews. That of Dunkeld Cathedral shows what appears to be a kilt and plaid. (Might not this kilt be the 'half plaid' mentioned in 1645 and shown on the map of Aberdeen, 1661, and in the Leys crest?) 1698

The Rev. James Brome mentions that Elgin is the chief city of the Highlanders where they go 'habited in mantles striped . . . about their shoulders . . . a coat girt close to their bodies and commonly are naked 1700 upon their legs but wear sandals. . . .' From Kirk Session and Town Council Minutes it is known that the inhabitants generally wore English clothes, often with the plaid, but it is interesting in showing that here the belted plaid was also worn.

1703   A Captain Hamilton wrote from Inverness to the Governor of Fort William: 'There is a match of Hunting to be as is said against 2nd of next month amongst several of our great folks, particularly the Duke of Hamilton is to be there, the Marquis of Atholl and an neighbour the Laird of Grant, who has ordered 600 of his men in arms, in good order, with tartane coats all of one colour and fashion. This is his order to the people of Straithspey.' And in the *Court Books of the Regality of Grants* appears: 'The said Ronal MakDonald of Gelloway and Archibald Mak-Donald of Tulloch Crombie, Wassels of Lagan in Badenoch, to the Right Hon. Ludovick Grant of that ilk and the tannantes and indwellers on these landis, are ordained to have readie tartans short coates and trewes and short hose of red and grein set dyce, all broad springed.' The Court of the Lands of Tulchine and Skeiradvey states: 'The Master to outrig the servantes in the said coates, trewes and hose out of their fies.' Red and green are popular colours. The clergy of Aberdeen were forbidden to wear red and green in 1256. The modern Grant tartan contains blue stripes, as well as red and green.

These large hunts had been held from early times. It has always been the custom to wear the hunting garb at them. Here again, the greater chiefs are preferring their men to wear tartans of the same pattern on such occasions. Livery was prominent in the cities, and it is only natural that these chiefs should want their followers dressed alike. If clan tartans had then been prominent, the men of Tulchine and Skeiradvey, who were MacDonalds, would hardly have wanted to wear the Grant tartan. And it is unlikely that Grant would have described the tartan he wanted. He would have said: 'Short coates and trewes and short hose of *my* tartan.'

4TH DUKE OF PERTH

The tartans worn are not the same as those worn by the Third Duke shown on page 59

56

An examination of the Grant family portraits of that time shows that a great variety of tartans was worn. This is the same with other families, such as MacDonald of Armidale, Campbell, Sutherland, MacDonnell, MacLeod, Drummond, MacPherson, Fraser. However it is only reasonable to assume that it is from these occasional desires to have one's followers dressed alike that the 'clan' and 'family' tartans grew into being.

1703   It is known from Martin's *Western Isles* that tartans were beginning to take on certain characteristics in different districts. But to what extent it is impossible to judge. And in judging it must be remembered that a clan was closely related to the land on which it lived. In fact Scotland consisted of a large number of 'tiny Celtic provincial states or clan territories, which together formed the Realm of Scotland' (Innes of Learney, *Tartans of the Clans*). Martin was a native of Skye, a tutor to MacLeod's children, and also to those of MacDonald of Sleat. He wrote in detail on the costume of the Islands and it does seem that if each clan had its own tartan he would have stated this fact. He does, however, mention a connection between tartan and 'place of residence'.

His description makes a suitable end to this section. The eighteenth century saw tartan rising as the symbol of Scotland and the badge of those who fought for her independence. And it is a fitting summary of the progress of the costume from early times to this period.

'The first habit wore by Persons of Distinction in the Islands was the Leni-Croich, from the Irish word Leni, which signifies a Shirt, and Croch, Saffron, because their Shirt was dyed with that Herb: the ordinary number of Ells used to make this Robe was twenty-four: it was the upper Garb, reaching below the knees, and was tied with a Belt round the middle; but the Islanders have laid it aside about a hundred years ago.

3RD DUKE OF PERTH (1713–1746) By F. de Troy
He died on his way to France after the battle of Culloden. He wears the plaid with tartan trews, a form of the costume favoured more by the nobility at that time. The tartans do not correspond with those in the portrait of the Fourth Duke of Perth, shown on page 57

58

'They now generally use Coat, Wastcoat, and Breeches, as elsewhere; and on their Heads wear Bonnets made of thick Cloth, some blew, some black and some gray.

'Many of the People wear Trowis, some of them very fine Waven, like Stockings of those made of Cloath; some are coloured, and others striped; the latter are as well shap'd as the former, lying close to the Body from the middle downwards, and tied round with a belt above the Haunches. There is a square piece of Cloth which hangs down before. The measure for shaping the Trowis is a stick of wood, whose length is a cubit, and that divided into the length of a finger, and half a finger: so that it requires more skill to make it, than the ordinary habit.

'The shoes antiently wore, were a piece of the hide of a deer, cow or horse, with the hair on, being tied behind and before with a point of leather. The generality now wear shoes, having one thin sole only, and shaped after the right and left foot; so that what is for one foot will not serve the other.

'But persons of distinction wear the Garb in fashion in the South of Scotland.

'The plad wore only by the men, is made of fine wool, the thred as fine as can be made of that kind; it consists of divers colours, and there is a great deal of ingenuity required in sorting the colours, so as to be agreeable to the nicest fancy. For this reason the women are at great pains, first to give an exact pattern of the plad upon a piece of wood, having the number of every thred of the stripe on it. The length of it is commonly seven double ells; the one end hangs by the Middle over the left arm, the other going round the body, hangs by the end over the left arm also: the right hand above it is to be at liberty to do any thing upon occasion. Every isle differs from each other in their fancy of making plads, as to the stripes in Breadth, and colours. This humour is as different through the main land of the Highlands, in-so-far that they who have seen those places, are able, at the first view of a man's plad, to guess the place of his residence.

'When they travel on foot, the plad is tied on the breast with a bodkin

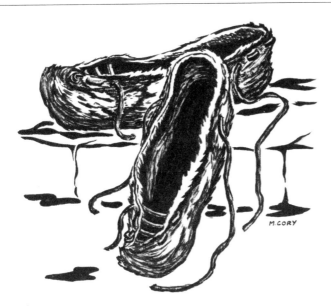

CUARANS

'The shoes antiently wore, were a piece of the hide of a deer, cow
or horse, with the hair on, being tied behind and before with a
point of leather.' Martin Martin's *Western Isles*, 1703

of bone or wood (just as the spira wore by the Germans, according to the
description of C. Tacitus): the plad is tied round the middle with a leather
belt: it is pleated from the belt to the knee very nicely: this dress for foot-
men is found much easier and lighter than breeches or trowis.'

If one is right in assuming that Martin here refers to clan tartans as they
are known today, we yet have evidence in later years that they had become by no means general. It seems more likely from what he says that
the colours of the plaids were either restricted by the dyes available in the
locality — thus controlling the colours that could be used — or that they
were rather more on a district basis than actually clan or family tartans.

JAMES MORAY OF ABERCAIRNY (1705–1777) By Jeremiah
Davison, *c.* 1739

This is an excellent picture showing the belted plaid, the 'kilt' being
the lower part of the plaid. The tartans worn are unknown today
and different from those in the picture on page 73

CHAPTER FOUR

Tartan — the Symbol of Scotland

RELENTLESSLY THAT 'culture' of the Lothians has been shooting out its long tentacles. Even in the remote Islands the 'Persons of Distinction wear the Garb in fashion in the South'. It seemed as if tartan, in any of the forms in which it was worn, was soon to become a thing of the past.

But the Union of Scotland and England was now to take place. This would bring great commercial advantages and thus, to a large extent, was popular with those who lived in towns. But by many of the people in the country districts it was resented and a great surge of nationalism rose through the land. Tartan became the symbol of those who fought to preserve the independence of Scotland.

During the last century a cleavage had gradually grown between those who could benefit from the trading in the towns and the advantages which this brought, and those who inhabited the more remote parts of the kingdom. Poor communications, 'difficult' soil and unfavourable weather were not conducive to trade which would have attracted the traders and so brought those advantages. 'Conditions varied according to circumstances — distance of the Estate from the Lowlands, the physical nature of the country,' writes John Mason in 'Conditions in the Highlands after the 'Forty-five', *Scottish Historical Review*, October, 1947.

From their remote glens, living in poverty and often in near starvation, these inhabitants felt envious as they watched the rest of the people grow more affluent. This envy soon became tinged with jealousy. They adopted a 'false' pride, despising the commercially minded townsman, and farmer, and tended to shut themselves off all the more from any contact with them. 'It is urged against it (the Highland dress)', wrote Capt. Burt in 1726, 'that it distinguishes the native as a body of people distinct and separate from the rest of the subjects of Great Britain, and thereby is one cause of their narrow adherence among themselves, to the exclusion of all

the rest of the kingdom... A few shillings will buy this dress for an ordinary Highlander, who, very probably, might hardly be in condition to purchase a Lowland suit, though of the coarsest cloth or stuff, fit to keep him warm in that cold climate.'

An ardent pride was taken in wearing the Scottish dress and, whilst it had diminished in the Lowland districts, its usage in the Highlands had become stronger. But tartan had certainly not lost its hold in the towns. It was not only worn by the poor, but was used for many things. Sir   1704 John Foulis of Ravelston, just west of Edinburgh, bought 'a tartan plaid to be a horss sheit' and Rachel Gordon wrote a postscript to her letter from Abergeldie, near Braemar, to her husband who was in Edinburgh: 1705 'My dear, with all the trouble you have buy me an apron of coloured Irish [Highland] tartan or cailigo.' It was not thought incongruous to write to a Lowland town for Highland tartan. And Lady Grisell Baillie of   1707 Jerviswood bought a plaid for her maid Meg Mill.

But some contacts had to be made by the Highlanders with those in the towns, and this glimpse by Defoe, writing from Edinburgh, sums up   1706 their attitude: 'They are all gentlemen, will take affront from no man, and insolent to the last degree. But certainly the absurdity is ridiculous to see a man in his mountain habit, armed with a broadsword, target, pistoll, at his girdle a dagger, and staff, walking down the High Street as upright and haughty as if he were a lord and withal driving a cow.' To a Southron this may appear unusual but at that time most small lairds did their own farm work.

Then came the Act of Union. It brought trade and prosperity to the   1707 Lowlander and some Highlanders were not slow to take advantage. At the Fair of Crieff, John Macky writes in his *Journey through Scotland*: 'There were at least thirty thousand Cattle sold there, most of them to

HALKERSTON OF RATHILLET IN FIFE (Artist unknown)
He wears a coat and plaid of tartans unknown today. His bonnet bears the Jacobite white cockade. This portrait was painted soon after the Rebellion of 1745

English Drovers, who paid down above thirty thousand Guineas in ready Money to the Highlanders; a sum they had never seen before, and proves one good effect of the Union.'

1709 But one cannot blame those who objected to the Union on the score that Scotland would lose its identity when the Commissioners for Clothing of the Army referred to Scotland thus: 'Your Commrs. observe there is a peculiar Cloathing for the Three Highland Companies in North Britain, not at all Military but like the Cloathing of the Natives there.' And the manufacture of tartan was becoming an excellent export. *The*
1711 *Present State of Scotland* tells us: 'It's proper to mention their Plaids, a Manufacture wherein they exceed all Nations, both as to Colour and Fineness. They have of late been pretty much fancy'd in England, and are very ornamental as well as durable for Beds, Hangings, Window-Curtains and Night-Gowns for Men and Women...A good improvement may be made of this manufacture for domestick use and export, now that the prohibition is remov'd by the Union.' In the Town Council Minutes of Elgin appears: 'Rates of Pettie Customes of the Burgh of Elgin...ilk elne tartane 4d.'

1713 'The first military body, under Government control, to adopt tartan as a part of their uniform was not, as might have been expected, a Highland regiment, but a Lowland one... The Royal Company of Archers in 1713 adopted a red tartan sett for their uniform. The first Highland regiment to wear tartan was the famous Black Watch (42nd), raised in 1729,' F. Adam reminds us in his *Clans, Septs and Regiments of the Scottish Highlands*. The portraits of those times show us that the tartan worn by the Royal Company of Archers was later changed to a green tartan.

1715 George Keith, 10th Earl Marischal of Scotland, in his *Memoirs* mentions the interesting fact that men used to throw away their plaids when charging into battle: 'Next morning, the Duke of Marr, finding most of our left had run away and was not returned, retired towards Perth, as the enemy had already done into Stirling; he resolved there to reassemble those who had run away, and although a considerable number of them were there before us, yet they were of no use having lost their cloaths in

68

(a)

(b)

(c)

ARCHERY MEDALS

(*a*) Alexander MacLeod of Muiravonside 1735; (*b*) Alexander Bayne of
Rirachies 1745; (*c*) David, Master of Northesk, Lord Rosehill, 1719.
The first military body, under Government control, to adopt tartan as a
part of their uniform was not, as might have been expected, a Highland regiment, but a Lowland one. The Royal Company of Archers in
1713 adopted a red tartan

the actions. To explain this, one must know the habits of the Highlanders and their manner of fighting. Their cloaths are composed of two short vests, the one above reaching only to the waste, the other about six inches longer, short stockings which reaches not quite to the knee and no breetches; but above all they have another piece of the same stuff, of about six yards long, which they tie about them in such a manner that it covers their thighs and all their body when they please, but commonly it's fixed on their left shoulder, and leaves their right arm free. This kind of mantell they throw away when they are ready to engage, to be lighter and less encumber'd and if they are beat it remains on the field, as happened to our left wing.'

1715   'The provost [of Glasgow] represented that being informed that upon severall occasions their Royal Highnesses the Prince and Princess of Wales had expressed their affection to the town of Glasgow and their speciall notice of and regaird to every token and evidence of affection and duty from this city, it was therefore judged not improper to send to her Highness a swatch of plaids as the manufactory peculiar only to this place for keeping the place in her Highness remembrance...and that accordingly he had sent home pairs of the best plaids which the place afforded at the tyme.'

A letter was sent with them in which it said: 'We humbly presume herewith to offer to your Highness by our member of Parliament, a swatch of one of the manufacturys peculiar to this place, being that of plaids which are generally used over that pairt of the United Kingdom called Scotland, by our women for covers when they go abroad, and by some men for the morning guns, or for hangins in bedrooms.' The member replied: 'This day I presented the plaides to the Princess. She was extremely pleased.'

1717   Again evidence of a preference for certain patterns is given in a letter dated from the Manse of Comrie, although it is rather against than for the argument for clan tartans. 'I give your lady hearty thanks for the highland plaid. It's good cloath but it does not answer the sett I sent some time agoe with McArthur.'

ILLUSTRATION FROM DEFOE'S *LIFE OF DUNCAN CAMPBELL*, SECOND EDITION, 1720

'Our young boy, now between six and seven, delighted in wearing a little bonnet and plaid, thinking it looked very manly in his countryman.'

1720   Tartan was growing as an export. Writes Pennant: 'At length a woollen manufacture arose in some degree. There was an exportation of it into Holland till 1720: it was a coarse kind, such as is made in the High-lands: much of it was sold to Glasgow, and sent into America for blankets for the Indians. It is in Scotland a clothing for the country people, and is worth about 10d or 12d a yard.'

1720   Defoe in his *Life of Duncan Campbell* states the average Scot's attitude to the dress in those days: 'Our young boy, now between six and seven, delighted in wearing a little bonnet and plaid, thinking it looked very manly in his countryman.' This boy then lived in London.

1723   The gentlemen found the belted plaid a little too primitive for society and were 'dressed in their slash'd, short Waistcoats, a Trousing (which is Breeches and Stockings of one piece of strip'd Stuff) with a Plaid for a Cloak, and a blue Bonnet' (*A Journey Through Scotland*).

It is interesting to note that the nobility, who had tended in even the most remote parts to wear the English dress, were adopting the Scottish again. 'The unpopularity of the Act of Union, however, in the period prior to the Forty-Five, had nursed a growing nationalism which ex-pressed itself in the wearing of Highland dress.' (G. F. Collie, *Highland Dress*, 1948.)

1726   Captain Burt in his *Letters from the Highlands* refers to this: 'The plaid is the undress of the ladies [at Inverness] and to a genteel woman who adjusts it with a good air, it is a becoming veil. But as I am pretty sure you never saw one of them in England, I shall employ a few words to describe it to you. It is made of silk or fine worsted, chequered with various lively colours, two breaths wide, and three yards in length; it is brought over the head, and may hide or discover the face according to the wearer's fancy or occasion; it reaches to the waist behind; one corner falls as low as the ancle on one side and the other part in folds hangs down from the opposite arm. . . . I have been told in Edinburgh that the ladies distinguish their political principles, whether Whig or Tory, by the manner of wear-ing their plaids.'

c. 1729   He describes the trews and plaid worn by Highland gentlemen and

72

THE MACDONALD BOYS (Artist unknown)

It will be seen that the boys are wearing different tartans, all unknown today

JAMES FRANCIS EDWARD MORAY, eldest son of the 13th Laird of Abercairny
By Jeremiah Davison

The tartan worn is not the same as that shown in the picture facing page 62

COUNTRY GIRL
WEARING PLAID From
McIan's *Costumes of the Clans*

'Many women wear,
especially the meaner sort,
plaids . . . which is cast over
their heads, and covers their
faces on both sides, and
would reach almost to the
ground.' Sir William
Brereton, 1636

adds: 'To a well-proportioned man, with any tolerable air, it makes an agreeable figure; but this you have seen in London, and it is chiefly their mode of dressing when in the Lowlands, or when they make a neighbouring visit or go any where on horseback; but those among them who travel on foot, and have not attendants to carry them over the waters, vary it into the quilt [kilt].' The kilt is certainly excellent for fording burns and rivers and striding through wet heather. Perhaps the following explains its unpopularity as a town dress: 'For the most part they wear the petticoat so very short, that in a windy day, going up a hill, or stooping, the indecency of it is plainly discovered.'

Allan Ramsay's poems and plays confirm the general use of tartan and that the people considered it to be the national costume of Scotland. He describes a Lowland shepherd as wearing:

> 'A tartan plaid spun o'gude hawslock woo,
> Scarlet and green the sets, the borders blue,
> Wi' sprangs like gowd and siller, crossed wi' black.'

> 'I am gawn to seek a wife
> I am gawn to buy a plaidy.'

> 'Oh, first of garb, garment of happy fate
> So long employed, of such an antique date,
> Look back some thousands years till records fail,
> And lose themselves in some romantic tale;
> We'll find our God-like fathers nobly scorned
> To be by any other dress adorned.'

The Rev. John Skinner wrote in 'The Christmas Ba'in' of Monymusk': 1739

> 'A stalwart stirk in tartan claise,
> Sware mony a sturdy aith,
> To bear the ba' thro' a' his faes
> An' nae hape muckle skaith.'

How is the export of tartan doing? From the *Caledonian Mercury* we read: '14 Jan.: Last Saturday the Agatha and Jane, Thomas Christie 1740

continued on page 78

75

ILLUSTRATION FROM BURT'S *LETTERS FROM THE NORTH*, c. 1730

The four Highlanders are shown, except the second from the left, wearing their trews. Two are wearing their plaids drawn over their shoulders in the way a modern shawl might be worn

LES ECOSSAIS A PARIS OU LA CURIOSITE DES FEMMES By Genty, 1815

'For the most part they wear the petticoat so very short, that in a windy day, going up a hill, or stooping, the indecency of it is plainly discovered.' Captain Burt, 1726

continued from page 75

cleared out from Leith for London, having on board the following Scots manufactures, viz., 53,381 yards of Linen, 3,006 yards of Tartans.' 'Leith, 18 Feb.: The Edinburgh Merchant, John Dick, cleared out for London with the following Scots manufactures, viz., 41,400 yards of Linen, 6,400 yards of Tartan.'

1742   *The Statistical Account of Kilwinning* (Ayr) says: 'The wives of some of the more wealthy and substantial farmers and tradesmen had silk plaids: but by far the greater part of the married women, red or striped worsted ones. Young women wore woollen cloaks, with hoods of the same kind of cloth. . . . The women in general seldom put on shoes and stockings.'

In the Rising of 1745, the tartan and the wearing of national dress rose to its greatest popularity. Hitherto it had been worn chiefly in the form of a belted-plaid, but now the modern type of kilt comes much more on the scene. That is the plaid and the lower part which formed the kilt are now separate. It may have been that the warriors, who when entering battle used to throw away the belted plaid to give themselves more freedom (see 1715) had found this uneconomical and left them in an attire hardly suitable for the age in which they now lived! Or it may have been the influence of that 'culture'. The kilt certainly became longer and now generally reached the knee. In some instances it was even drawn between the legs to form voluminous shorts.

In the picture of the battle of Culloden, executed at the time by A. Heckel, and in that of Alexander Monro, the piper to Prince Charles Edward, the kilt is shown drawn between the legs in this fashion. The supporters of the MacPherson coat of arms are dressed the same and Alexander Nisbett, the great herald, describes it: 'their shirts tied between them'. The painting of Sir Stuart Threipland of Fingask, by Delacour, painted about this period, also shows this style.

UNKNOWN LADY By William Mosman
'The plaid is the undress of the ladies and to a genteel woman who adjusts it with a good air, it is a becoming veil.' Captain Burt in his *Letters from the Highlands*, 1726

DETAIL FROM BATTLE OF CULLODEN (*b*)

About this time the lower part of the belted plaid is often shown
drawn between the legs. The supporters of the MacPherson coat of arms
are dressed the same. Alexander Nisbett in 1722 describes it 'their shirts
tied between them'

BATTLE OF CULLODEN, 1745 By A. Heckel (*a*)

This picture of the battle scene was probably made from official
observation

The Jacobite army was fighting for independence and it wore the old costume of Scotland. There was no distinction between Highlander or Lowlander. Home, an eye-witness of the times, wrote: 'When the rebels began their march to the Southward, they were not 6,000 men complete; they exceeded 5,500, of whom 400 or 500 were cavalry; and of the whole number, not quite 4,000 were real Highlanders, who formed the clan regiments, and were indeed the strength of the rebel army. All the regiments of foot wore the Highland garb, they were thirteen in number, many of them very small.' Sir Walter Scott confirms this: 'They marched in two divisions, of which the first, commanded by Lord George Murray, comprehended what are called the Lowland regiments; although the greater part so called Lowland were Highland by language and all of them by dress, the Highland garb being the uniform of all the infantry of the Jacobite army.' Ewan MacPherson of Cluny, Chief of the Clan Mac-Pherson, wrote in his *Memoirs*: 'My Lord George Murray, being dressed en montagnard, as all the army were, lost his bonnet and wig. . . .' David, Lord Ogilvy, who commanded Ogilvy's Horse is depicted in a half-length painting wearing a red and blue tartan coat and a more elaborate plaid.

Donald Farquaharson of Auchriachan (Glenlivet), writing from Inver-cauld to Colonel James Moir of Stonnywood at Aberdeen, asks: 'If you want any Highland plaids or tartans for the men acquaint me, and I will endeavour to provide some.' There seems to be no worry about the correct tartan and indeed it seems very definite that clan tartans were not yet common in spite of the occasional references to chieftains dressing their men alike. And the following account by Mr Ray, a volunteer, rather confirms this: 'In the fight I came up with a pretty young High-lander, who called out to me: "Hold your hand — I am a Campbell!" On which I asked him: "Where's your bonnet?" "Somebody has snatched it off my head." I mention this to show how we distinguished our loyal clans from the rebels, they being dressed and equipped all in one way, except the bonnet; our having a red or yellow cross or ribbon,

continued on page 85

SIR STUART THREIPLAND OF FINGASK By William Delacour

Sir Stuart is seen to be wearing his plaid after the fashion of the soldiers at Culloden.
A portrait of Alexander Monro, the piper to Prince Charles Edward, shows the kilt also
drawn between the legs

LORD OGILVY By Allan Ramsay

David, Lord Ogilvy, commanded Ogilvy's Horse in the Jacobite army, 1745.
He was attainted and subsequently pardoned on account of his youth

continued from page 82

their's a white cockade. He having neither of these distinctions, I desired him, if he was a Campbell to follow me, which he promised: but on the first opportunity he gave me the slip.'

When the Manchester Regiment was formed by the adherents to the Jacobite cause 'both officers and men wore white cockades, and the authority of the colonel was indicated by the addition of a tartan sash' — so wrote Robert Chambers in his *History of the Rebellion.* 'Jemmy Dawson', a ballad by W. Skenstone, recalls how James Dawson of Manchester rose for the cause and was executed on July 30th, 1746:

> 'But curse on party's hateful strife
> That led the faithful youth astray.
> The day the rebel clans appeared
> O, had he never seen that day.
> 'Their colours and their sash he wore
> And in the fatal dress was found;
> And now he must that death endure
> Which gives the brave the keenest wound.'

'Mr Buchnay, provost of Linlithgow in 1745, was a keen Jacobite . . . When the Highland army drew near, the provost fled towards Edinburgh; but his wife and daughters remained, and waited upon the Prince, with tartan gowns and white cockades.' (*Jacobitism Triumphant,* 1753.) 'Gairdner and Taylor . . . Lawn-market, Edinburgh, continue to sell . . . at lowest Rates, great Choice of Tartans, the newest Patterns, Cotton Checks and Sarges, of which they are also Makers.' *Caledonian Mercury,* 4 October, 1745. It seems that tartans, whether clan or not, were still being designed.

Then came the day of retribution: Aikmen in his *History* tells us that Arthur Elphinstone, Lord Balmerino, was executed in London: 'drawing on a flannel waistcoat, which he had provided, as he said, for his shroud, he added the last piece of dress, a tartan night cap, affirming that he died a Scottishman', and from Robert Chambers we learn that 'Nicholson had kept a coffee-house at Leith and was a man in middle life, but MacDonald

1746

continued on page 90

85

PRINCE CHARLES EDWARD
He does not seem to have worn the kilt before the battle of Culloden, but he is
often depicted wearing a plaid, the tartans differing greatly. He did wear the
kilt when he was hiding in the Highlands

REBELLION REWARDED, 1746

Some of the figures are wearing belted plaids, some tartan plaids over ordinary dress. It will be noted that those who wear the belted plaid have the lower part pulled between the legs. This method of wearing the costume is often shown in pictures of this period

THE BELTED PLAID From
McIan's *Costumes of the Clans*
The belted plaid was the
tartan plaid as an outer
garment covering the whole
body and gathered at the
waist to form a full skirt
reaching to the knees

DETAILS OF HIGHLAND TROOPS AT MAINZ, 1743

Left: The top part of the belted plaid is being thrown over the left shoulder
Right: The belted plaid is worn over both shoulders as a protection from the rain

continued from page 85

and Ogilvie were both young men of good families, the first a cadet of the family of Keppock, and the other a native of the county of Banff . . . MacDonald and Nicholson appeared at the last solemn scene [execution in London] in their Highland Dress'.

It is significant that the Act forbidding the wearing of tartan, when speaking of arms, mentions: 'within the shire of Dunbartain, on the North Side of the Water of Leven, Stirling on the North Side of the River of Forth, Perth, Kincardin, Aberdeen, Inverness, Nairn, Cromarty, Argyle, Forfar, Bamff, Sutherland, Caithness, Elgine and Ross' and when speaking of tartan: 'within that part of Great Britain called Scotland'.

It is in this Act that the first reference to the 'Philebeg or little kilt' appears. The little kilt means the kilt separate from the plaid. A song of this time called 'Though Geordie Reigns in Jamie's Stead' also mentions 'the tartan hose and philabeg'.

The *Forfeited Estates Papers* tells how the inhabitants of Strathgartney, near Callendar, tried to get round the Act by wearing 'short blue cloath coats or other short coats of one colour in place of Tartan, and Trousers of one colour resembling the little kilts, with this difference, that they were sewed up the middle'. Tobias Smollett, in *Humphrey Clinker,* says: 'They are compelled to wear breeches; a restraint which they cannot bear with any degree of patience: indeed, the majority wear them not in their proper place, but on poles or longstaves over their shoulders.'

1747   Duncan Forbes of Culloden, 'the wisest observer of the times', wrote: 'It is remarkable that in some districts *bordering on the Highlands* where within memory the inhabitants spoke the Irish Language, wore the Highland dress, and were accustomed to make use of Arms, upon the accidental introduction of industry, the Irish Language and Highland dress gave way to a sort of English, and Lowland Cloathing; the inhabitants took to the Plough in place of Weapons, and tho' disarmed by no Act of Parliament are as tame as their Low Country neighbours.' Alasdair MacDhonnachaidh Ruaidh speaks of the dress as 'the garments of the hill'.

SIR ROBERT DALRYMPLE OF CASTLETON (Artist unknown)

Tartan was worn by Lowland Whig families as well as by Highland Jacobite families, as witness the portrait of the Laird of North Berwick's son, Sir Robert Dalrymple, who was married in the year of the Union

BLACK WATCH From *The Cloathing Book* drawn up by the War Office, 1742

The first Highland regiment to wear tartan was the famous Black Watch (42nd), raised in 1729. It was called 'Black Watch' after its dark tartan

1748   It was sometime before the Act of 1746 could be carried out, and the General Orders to the Army in Scotland in 1748 stated: 'By the Act passed last session of Parliament, the time for the general abolishing the Highland dress is enlarged to the 1st day of August, 1749. But that the wearing and use of such parts thereof as are called the plaid, philibeg, or little kilt, is absolutely prohibited and abolished from and after the 25th day of this instant December, and as to these particulars the law takes place from that day.' It appears the Act was not strictly adhered to in the South or by those who were adherents of the Government. Many portraits were painted during this time, showing various tartans unknown today and varying quite freely in the same family.

The Statistical Account of Scotland gives many accounts of the change that took place in dress: Bathgate (Linlithgow): 'The alteration in dress since 1750 is also remarkable. When the good man and his sons went to kirk, market, wedding, or burial, they were clothed in a home spun suit of freezed cloth, called kelt (a kind of black cloth), pladden hose, with a blue or brown bonnet; and the good wife and her daughters were dressed in gowns and petticoats of their own spinning, with a cloth cloak and hood of the same, or a tartan of red plaid. But now (1792) the former, when they go abroad, wear suits of English cloth, good hats, etc., and the latter the finest printed cottons, and sometimes silk gowns, silk caps, and bonnets of different shapes, sizes and colours, white stockings, cloth shoes, etc.' Kilsyth (Stirling): 'The females formerly wore nothing but a linen head dress and tartan worsted plaids, which covered the head or at best red scarlet cloaks.' Wigton: 'The old dress of the country men, even of the most respectable farmers, a kilt coat, a blue bonnet, and plaiding hose, have been totally laid aside . . . The old dress, too, of the country women, even of the farmers' wives and daughters, the blue cloth cloaks and hoods; the tartan or red plaides and the worsted gowns and aprons of

THE HIGHLAND WEDDING By Jacob de Witt (*fl.* 1684–1686)
Several of the men are wearing tartan trews. The plaid is being worn by some of the men and women

A LOWLAND WEDDING By Jacob de Witt (*fl.* 1684–1686)

The costume is very similar to that shown in 'The Highland Wedding' although no men are shown wearing tartan trews. Several of the men and women are wearing plaids

their own spinning, are also gone almost wholly into disuse.' Mid-Calder (Edinburgh): 'The tartan or red plaids . . . constituted the dress of women in the inferior conditions of life. . . .'

And tartan is still manufactured. The Town Council Minutes of Elgin state in the Rate of the Petty Customs of the Burgh: 'Ilk barred or plain plaid nine elns and upwards, little and heel spun 1s 6d. Ilk tartan bed or blanket nine elns and upwards big and heel spun 1s.' And the *Edinburgh Evening Courant* carries these advertisements. 'There is to be sold by roup in the shop of William Watson in the front of the New Exchange of Edinburgh upon Monday, 3rd day of March next the whole goods which belonged to the said William Watson consisting of Tartans of all kinds, poplins, durants, calicoes . . .' and 'James Baillie, Merchant in Edinburgh, has removed his warehouse to the Exchange fronting the Tron where Tartans or Plaids with other goods are sold as formerly.' 1752 1760

That the kilt was considered the costume of the Highlander only is again refuted by Ivan Baillie of Aberiachan: '. . . this piece of dress . . . was . . . in our Scots termed little kilt: and it was found so handy and convenient that, in the shortest space, the use of it became frequent in all the Highland Countries and in many of our northern Low Countries also.' He was writing of the probable origin of the philabeg which had only recently come into use. 1768

Pennant in his *Tour Through Scotland* shows how great had the manufacture of tartan grown: Stirling 'has a manufacture of tartanes' and also Kilmarnock. These may have been for export only, or for the army. Of Langholme (Dumfries) he says: 'The manufactures are stuffs, serges, black and white plaids.' These black and white plaids —hodden grey or shepherd's tartan —were becoming very popular now throughout Scotland, having been introduced into the Highland districts by Lowland shepherds. 1772

The Act of 1746 was repealed in 1782. For thirty-five years tartan had been forbidden in 'that part of Great Britain called Scotland'. Leniency had been shown in the South —and it must be remembered that the Act only prevented men and boys from wearing tartans, not women —and to a 1782

95

few in the North who were adherents to the Government — by no means to all adherents — but thirty-five years is a long time. Long enough for the dress to be considered as that of a past generation. If it had not been used by the Highland Regiments during these years, it might never again have been worn. But these regiments, adding glory to Scotland's history, kept the old national garb before the eyes of the people. Upon the repeal of the Act, tartan was resumed again but never to the degree of former times. The hodden grey 'maud' (plaid) was generally its present form but, little by little, a national feeling turned the people to the symbol of Scotland and its adoption largely in the shape of plaids. The kilt was worn on ceremonious occasions or as a convenient garb for hunting by the gentry. The poor man could not afford to buy such an elaborate costume since his wife no longer spun and weaved.

1793 *The Statistical Account of Scotland* gives us little glimpses here and there of the resumption of the homely tartan plaid by the women, always more conservative than men: Forfar, Kirkden (Angus), Cres (Fife), Symington (Ayr), Montquhitter (Aberdeen) Mains of Fintry (Forfar), Duffus (Moray), Ardclach (Nairne), Bannockburn, Logie (Forfar), Coupar of Angus, Forglen (Banff), Kintore (Aberdeen). At Athelstaneford (Haddington) 'a woollen manufacture of striped variegated cloth has been carried on in the village for some years past on a small scale'. At Doune (Perth), sporrans are made. At Barrie, ladies' Sabbath day plaids cost 'when dyed of two or three various colours and containing about 4 yards' 16/- a piece; hodden 'is mostly used for herds' cloaks and is sold at 1/8d the yard': Dowally, near Dunkeld, had not in 1778 '4 houses in the parish where tea was used. . . . Then many of the men wore the philibeg; now there are none who do so. Then, all of them had tartan hose; now all have stockings. . . .' At Leochel 'the men dress plainly in short clothes and breeches of homespun cloth, with tartan or shepherds plaids. . . . The

HIGHLAND CHIEFS From James Logan's *The Scottish Gael*, 1831
This beautiful hand-painted picture formed the frontispiece of *The Scottish Gael*, by James Logan, 1831. It shows the plaid and kilt as separate garments

96

women appear at church as decently dressed as their circumstances will permit, in tartan plaids and duffle cloaks.' At Petty, on the Firth of Moray, the dress 'is still retained by them in a great measure. The plaid is almost totally laid aside but the small blue bonnet, the short coat, the tartan kilt and hose, and the Highland brogues are still the ordinary dress of the men.'

These are but instances. In the country generally the dress had fallen out of usage. The change is summarized well in a typical lowland village, Campsie:

> '1714 — The men wore bonnets and plaids, with plaiding waistcoats and plaiding hose, no English cloth whatever was worn by the inhabitants, the gentry excepted.
>
> '1744 — No English cloth used by the inhabitants.
>
> '1759 — English cloth began to be worn occasionally by the better sort of people, along with worsted stockings, and buckles in their shoes.
>
> '1794 — Every lad now dresses in English cloth and fancy waistcoats, with thread or cotton stockings: and every girl in cotton stuff, black silk cloaks and fancy bonnets.'

And under the Parish of Meigle (East Perthshire) is written: 'Since the year 1745, a fortunate epoch for Scotland in general, improvements have been carried on with great ardour and success. At that time, the state of this country was rude beyond conception. . . . The common people, clothed in the coarsest garb and starving on the meanest fare, lived in despicable huts with their cattle.'

1822   It took a Sir Walter Scott to bring the garb back to some form of popularity. Under his direction, the Scottish nobility resumed this ancient dress on the occasion of the visit of King George IV to Edinburgh. His Majesty appeared resplendent in kilt and plaid and Sir Walter likewise. 'A great renaissance took place . . . there was a rush for kilts and tartans,' jibes Mackay in his *Romantic History of the Highland Garb*.

Fostered by the novels of Sir Walter, the efforts of Stewart of Garth, the paintings of Sir Henry Raeburn and by Queen Victoria herself, the

98

TWO SCOTTISH ROVERS UNDERGOING THEIR VIGIL

The old dress has come back to its earliest use — a dress for those who
roam the wild open moors and the steep rugged mountains

dress became widely adopted. Authors rushed into print, their judgments often marred by the word 'Highland', and 'Clan' and 'family' tartans were hastily designed from the flimsiest evidence — or sometimes even from pure imagination.

This desire to humanize and personalize the tartan was of great importance in strengthening the interest in tartan and as such is to be welcomed but it must be remembered that few, if any, clan or family tartans as worn today can claim any length of history in themselves and it is quite unwarranted to belittle any one tartan because it is thought not to be old — since it is very doubtful if any can claim this distinction.

But it is to the youth of Scotland that the dress chiefly appeals today. To them, the perpetual 'squabbles' and 'taboos' of the early Victorian theorists have little interest. To them it is a dress that is healthy and of which they are proud. It is of no importance to them when or where it should be worn. North, South, East and West we find them, striding the country roads, following the distant tracks, wearing the tartan — the symbol of Scotland. The old dress has come back to its earliest use — a dress for those who roam the wild open moors and the steep rugged mountains.

COLONEL ALASDAIR MACDONELL OF GLENGARRY (1771–1828)
By Sir Henry Raeburn

He lived outside the period dealt with in this book but the picture illustrates the attempt of some of the chieftains to revive the costume. It certainly makes a handsome figure

A Short Anthology

A SHOCKING DRESS:

'They [the women] never wear shoes or stockings but on Sunday. . . .
Strangers from the South . . . cry out against both as shocking pieces of
barbarity.'   *The Statistical Account of Scotland*, 1793

A SIMPLE DRESS:

'The wages allowed a man who can plow, sew, etc., is £6 sterling,
together with shoes and clothes: he is allowed 4 pair of single shoes,
commonly called Brogues, 2 pair of hose, 4 yards of tartan for a Phellibeg,
and a short coat and vest of some coarse kind of cloth.'
                                     The Statistical Account of Scotland, 1793

AN IDLER'S DRESS:

'It were much better for the people, and their country, that they had
never seen a village but had remained in the simplicity of rural life,
wrapped in their plaids all day long, as their fathers were, on the brow of
a hill, attending their cattle, and composing sonnets.'
                                     The Statistical Account of Scotland, 1793

COUNTRY DRESS:

'The ladies and gentlemen generally dress as in the low country; though,
when at home, some of the gentlemen wear the country dress; which is,
a bonnet, a short coat, a little kilt, or philebeg, tartan hose, and a plaid:
but the trouse and belted plaid never recovered their place since 1745.'
                                     The Statistical Account of Scotland, 1793

A HANDSOME DRESS:

'Tartans are highly esteemed and the colours are indeed so well dyed and intermingled with such taste that I can hardly conceive any fancy dress more becoming and handsome.'

Journey Through Scotland, R. HERON, 1793

AN IDEAL DRESS:

'The garb is certainly very loose and fits men inured to it to go through great marches, to bear out against the inclemency of the weather, to wade through rivers, to shelter in huts, woods, and rocks on occasions, which men dressed in the low country garb could not endure.'

Forbes of Culloden, 1747

AN INCONVENIENT DRESS:

'The highland dress is very common in this town and neighbourhood [Inverness], and is undoubtedly much more picturesque and beautiful than the formal, tight, stiff habit of the English and Europeans in general. The highland bonnet is in particular very ornamental; so are the graceful folds of the plaid: the modern habit has, however, convenience to recommend it, and in a few years this ancient dress of the highlanders which resembles very much that of the ancient Romans, will probably be scarcely seen.'   *Tour Through the Highlands*, T. GARNETT, 1800

LORD GLENORCHY By C. Jervis, *c.* 1708
The tartans worn are unknown today

THE ANCIENT DRESS:

'The ancient dress of the Highlanders is fast giving way to a more modern costume, although the ancient dress is still retained in many places, and often worn by gentlemen on particular occasions. It is formed by woollen stuff, chequered with different colours, well known by the name of tartan . . . The inhabitants of the low country more resemble the English . . . The plaid is in very general use, especially in the South country. The Lowland plaid, however, is different from the Highland in the checks being smaller, and the colours not so much variegated.'

Topographical Dictionary of Scotland, DAVID WEBSTER, 1817

A ROYAL DRESS:

'Besides the sovereign [George IV], many chieftains of clans, noblemen and gentlemen appeared in the highland garb among whom were observed the Dukes of Hamilton and Argyll, the Earl of Breadalbane, Lord Gwydir and Lord Glenorchy . . . Curtis also appeared in the same attire: and it was remarked, whenever his Majesty and the worthy alderman met, that neither could refrain from smiling — probably at the singularity of their appearance in the "garb of the Tartan Confederacy".'

Scotland Illustrated, DR WILLIAM BEATTIE, 1842

AN EXPENSIVE DRESS:

'It is customary with those who wear the kilt to wash their limbs at least every morning, and when one assumes this dress only occasionally, some recommend, as a preventative from catching cold, that the legs should be annointed with whisky.' *The Scottish Gael*, J. LOGAN, 1831

A PASTORAL DRESS:

'The belted plaid was, however, by no means unknown as a dress in

106

many parts accounted lowland by the natives of higher districts. It was peculiarly convenient for pastoral occupations and was the common dress of the shepherds in the inland parts of Aberdeen, Banff and other counties north of the Grampians until towards the end of the last century.'

The Scottish Gael, J. LOGAN, 1831

THE CHILDREN'S DRESS:

'In another great apartment of this house [Owen's 'feelosofers' at New Lanark], there were eighteen boys and eighteen girls, the boys dressed in Highland dresses, without shoes on, naked from three inches above the knee, down to the foot, a tartan plaid close round the body, in their shirt sleeves, their shirt collars open, each having a girl by the arm, duly proportioned in point of size, the girls without caps, and without shoes and stockings.'

Tour in Scotland, WILLIAM COBBETT, 1832

A USEFUL DRESS:

'We had gained about three quarters of a mile in advance of the mail when the torrent descended in all its fury. I wrapped my body in my plaid, thinking nothing of my legs which, being bare below my kilt, only required a rub to dry them.'

'If the angler be not well supplied with material for bodies of flies, I recommend him to examine the colours of his plaid or bonnet, if he wear such articles . . . I dressed some of my best killing flies with bodies supplied by my highland stockings and plaid.'

'On several occasions I met with extra kindness and civility, from my appearance in the Highland garb, when a parent uttered in Gaelic to his son, words, meaning in English — "Be kind, and show the best fishing places to the man in the kilt, and take care of him and bring him back in safety." '

Wandering by the Lochs and Streams, J. HICKS, 1854

A TREACHEROUS DRESS:

'Victoria is greatly distressed to find that Brown is suffering from dreadfully lacerated and swollen knees, caused by the flapping of his sodden kilt during the journey. He can hardly walk. The doctor is summoned. He is told he must rest.'   *Queen Victoria's John Brown*, E. E. P. TISDALL

AN UNRELIABLE DRESS:

'It is unwarrantable . . . to imagine Scotch extraction a sufficient guarantee that you will look well in a kilt.'   R. L. STEVENSON, 1880

A DECEPTIVE DRESS:

'At my school we used to play another school at cricket, and they worried us by playing the same boy in flannels for the 1st XI and in knickerbockers for the 2nd, and in a kilt for the 3rd. We could never quite prove it, but he was a great thorn in our side.'

Letter of J. M. BARRIE

A PATRIOT'S DRESS:

'A word or two on the wearing of the kilt, by no means the least important of the passions ruling the Colonel's life. During many of his years in retirement, the kilt formed his principal article of apparel. Trews thereunder were scorned, since the wearing of them was not in the true tradition. It denoted degeneracy. Only namby-pambies and alien shooting tenants, disporting tartans to which they had no right, wore these "undies". The kilt required no such unseen garment.'

The Turbulent Year, A. A. MACGREGOR

A PRINCE'S DRESS:

'He [Prince Charles] was barefooted, had an old black kilt coat on, phili-beg, and waistcoat, a dirty shirt, and a long red beard, a gun in his hand, a pistol and dirk by his side.'   *Journal*, JOHN CAMERON

'He saluted me kindly. . . . His dress was then a tartan short-coat and vest of the same, got from Lady Clanranald; his nightcap all patched with Soot-drop: his shirt, hands and face, patched with the same: a short kilt, tartan hose and Highland brogues.'   HUGH MACDONALD of Balshair

A HYGIENIC DRESS:

'Let him make the discovery that the kilt in Scotland is regarded chiefly as a hygienic garment for small boys.'
                The Badge of Scotland, DOUGLAS HAY SCOTT, 1935

A WARM DRESS:

'Southerners think the Scottish kilt a chilly garment, but with its layers of pleated cloth protecting the waist and abdomen it actually is not so.'
                The Lady, 24 January, 1946

A PRACTICAL DRESS:

'Personally, I usually don the Hunting Robertson tartan when on holiday in the Highlands. . . . The kilt or shorts can safely be classed as universal sporting garments today, in fact they are frequently favoured by Royalty. The kilt is a thoroughly utilitarian garment, and is probably the most practical garb for sport of all kind, particularly for rough fishing and shooting.'   *Angling in Wildest Scotland*, R. M. ROBERTSON

AN INDECENT DRESS:

'The men of St Kilda had curious notions of the wearing of the kilt. When the people of that island landed at Oban from the vessel which had brought them to the mainland [*c.* 1930] a well-known highlander of the district who had come to welcome them was thus addressed: "Are you not ashamed, you who have the Gaelic, to go about in so indecent a manner, with your knees exposed!"'

Highways and Byeways in the West Highlands, SETON GORDON, 1935

A SCHOOLBOY'S DRESS:

'In those Beith days I was hardy enough. I skated in a kilt, with very short trews and suffered nothing worse from the winter than chapped knees. . . . Nor was there any modern softness in the education provided at Seafield. Our life was Spartan. The east wind was a kill-or-cure tonic, and, as we wore the kilt, our knees and a part of our thighs were exposed to the full rigours of the cold. As a School dress the kilt is an admirable garment, but it has one disadvantage. Knees not washed properly after football are exposed to the full gaze of punctilious masters.'

My Scottish Youth, BRUCE LOCKHART

A NATIONAL DRESS:

'The tartan is not only to the Highlander, but also to the Lowland Scotchman, the emblem of his nationality. Any attempt, therefore, to disparage it or abolish the tartan awakes the ire and offends the sentiments of Highlanders and Lowlanders alike. . . . Ay, I venture to believe that all my readers of Scottish nationality will be willing to confess that, when our "heart does not warm to the tartan, it will be as cold as death can make it!"' *Clans, Septs and Regiments of the Scottish Highlands*, F. ADAM

O, THE ROAST BEEF OF OLD ENGLAND Part of Hogarth's *Gate of Calais*. Engraved by C. Mostey, 1749

It shows a full length figure of a Scotsman wearing a tartan jacket and trews. He wears a bonnet with the Jacobite white cockade

A POPULAR DRESS:

In giving a list of what visitors like to see most in Scotland, the Scottish Tourist Board (1948) placed second 'people wearing the kilt in the street'.

AN UNCHANGING DRESS:

'There have been few changes in the making of the kilt in the last two hundred years, although today the cloth is cut out at the waist to make a neater figure. Formerly this was not done, to permit of the kilt being turned four different times for reasons of economy. With the exception of regimental kilts, a kilt is always pleated to show the pattern of the tartan all round. The military style of box-pleating having one predominant stripe down each pleat is used only because it is more economical of material, and is not in accordance with the heraldic tradition of the tartan.' *Highland Dress*, GEORGE F. COLLIE, 1948

A BECOMING DRESS:

'The full dress of a dean is more becoming now than any other in vogue, except its one rival, the evening dress of a Scottish chieftain.'
GEORGE BERNARD SHAW

Bibliography

1808   *The Costume of Great Britain* by W. H. PYNE.

1822   *Sketches of the Characters of the Highlanders of Scotland* by STEWART OF GARTH.

1831   *The Scottish Gael* by JAMES LOGAN (Smith, Elder and Company).

1842   *Vestiarium Scoticum* by J. S. S. STUART and C. E. STUART (William Tate, Edinburgh).

1845   *The Clans of the Scottish Highlands* by R. R. MCIAN and JAMES LOGAN (Ackermann and Company).

1847   *Collectanea de Rebus Albanicis* (Iona Club).

1850   *The Clans of the Highlands of Scotland* by THOMAS SMIBERT (James Hogg, Edinburgh).

1850   *Authenticated Tartans of the Clans and Families of Scotland* by W. and A. SMITH (Mauchline, Ayrshire).

1850   *A History of the Highlands and of the Highland Clans* by JAMES BROWNE (A. Fullarton and Company, Edinburgh).

1870   *Highlanders of Scotland* by KENNETH MACLEAY (William Blackwood and Sons Limited, Edinburgh).

1872   *Clans and Tartans* (Tartans taken from W. and A. SMITH's book) (Andrew Elliot, Edinburgh).

1875   *A History of the Scottish Highlands, Highland Clans and Highland Regiments* by REV. T. MACLAUCHLAN (A. Fullarton and Company, Edinburgh).

1884   *Sketches of the Clans of Scotland* by CLANSMEN J.M.P., F.W.S. (Maclachlan and Stewart).

1886   *The Tartans of the Clans of Scotland* by JAMES GRANT (W. and A. K. Johnston Limited, Edinburgh).

1891   *The Scottish Clans and their Tartans* (W. and A. K. Johnston Limited, Edinburgh).

1893   *Old and Rare Scottish Tartans* by D. W. STEWART (George P. Johnston).

1895   *The Costumes of the Clans* by J. S. S. STUART and C. E. STUART (James Menzies).

1896   *What is My Tartan?* by FRANK ADAM (W. and A. K. Johnston Limited, Edinburgh).

1899   *Highland Dress, Arms and Ornament* by LORD ARCHIBALD CAMPBELL.

1901   *The Kilt* by S. R. ERSKINE.

1908   *Clans, Septs and Regiments of the Scottish Highlands* by FRANK ADAM (W. and A. K, Johnston Limited, Edinburgh).

1914   *The Kilt* by L. M. DOUGLAS.

1923   *The Highland Clans of Scotland* by G. E. TODD.

1924   *The Romantic Story of the Highland Garb and the Tartan* by J. G. MACKAY

1932   *Comunn an Fheilidh* (The Kilt Society).

1938   *Tartans of the Clans and Families of Scotland* by SIR THOMAS INNES OF LEARNEY (W. and A. K. Johnston Limited, Edinburgh).

1943   *Old Irish and Highland Dress* by H. F. MCCLINTOCK (W. Tempest, Dundalk).

1947   *Clans and Tartans of Scotland* by ROBERT BAIN (William Collins Sons and Company Limited, Glasgow).

1948   *Highland Dress* by GEORGE F. COLLIE and R. R. MCIAN (Penguin Books Limited, London).

1949   *Old Highland Dress and Tartans* by H. F. MCCLINTOCK and J. TELFER DUNBAR (W. Tempest, Dundalk).

1950   *The Setts of the Scottish Tartans* by D. C. STEWART (Oliver and Boyd Limited, Edinburgh).

1951   *Two Centuries of Highland Dress* by J. TELFER DUNBAR (Edinburgh Public Libraries and Museums Committee).

1957   *British Military Uniforms from Henry VII to Present Day* by W. Y. CARMAN.

1958   *Scottish Costume 1500–1850* by STUART MAXWELL and ROBIN HUTCHINSON (A. and C. Black Limited, London).

1960   *Tartans and Highland Dress* by C. R. MACKINNON (William Collins Sons and Company Limited, Glasgow).

1961   *Tartans* by CHRISTIAN HESKETH (Weidenfeld and Nicolson Limited, London).

1962   *History of Highland Dress* by J. TELFER DUNBAR (Oliver and Boyd Limited, Edinburgh).

Index of Sources

Aberdeen, Chartularies of, 12, 27, 39, 40, 42, 48, 56
Act of 1746, 4, 90, 92
Act of 1746 (repealed), 95, 96
Adam, F., *Clans, Septs and Regiments of the Scottish Highlands*, 7, 68, 110
Aikmen, James, *Continuation of Buchanan's History*, 85
d'Arfeville, Nicolay, 30
Armorial de Gelre, 14

Baillie, Lady Grisell, (accounts) 55, 67
Baillie of Aberiachan, Ivan, 95
Barrie, J. M. (letter), 108
Beattie, William, *Scotland Illustrated*, 106
Beauque, Jean de, 24
Brakeland, Jocelin of, *Chronicle*, 12
Brantôme, Pierre de, 24
Brereton, Sir William, *Diary*, 40
Brome, Rev. James, *Travels*, 55
Buchanan, George, *History of Scotland*, 7, 29
Burnett, Sir George, *The Family of Burnett of Leys*, 44, 46
Burt, Captain Edward, *Letters from the Highlands*, 65, 72

Caledonian Mercury, 75, 85
Camden, William, *Britannia*, 34
Cameron, John, *Journal*, 109
Cassius, Dio, 6
Chambers, Robert, *History of the Rebellion*, 85
Cobbett, William, *Tour in Scotland*, 107
Collectanea de Rebus Albanicis, Iona Club, Vol. I, 52
Collie, G. F., *Highland Dress*, 72, 112
Compostella, Guide to, 10
Comrie, Manse of, (letter) 70

Defoe, Daniel, *Life of Duncan Campbell*, 67, 72
Depradations, List of, 50
Diceto, Ralph de, *Imagines Historiarum*, 11
Drummond, James, *The Sculptured Monuments in Iona and the West Highlands*, 15
Dunbar, William, 15

Edinburgh Evening Courant, 95
Edinburgh, Provincial Council of, 21, 40, 43

Elder, John, (letter) 21
Elgin Burgh Court Book, 21, 30, 33, 37, 39, 42, 43, 44, 68, 95
Ethelredus of Rievallis, *De Bello Standardii*, 10
Eumenius, *Panegyric*, 6

Farquaharson of Auchriachan, Donald, (letter) 82
Forbes of Culloden, Duncan, 90, 104
Forfeited Estates Papers, 90
Foulis of Ravelston, Sir John, (accounts) 67
Franck, Richard, *Northern Memoirs*, 44

Garnett, T., *Tour Through the Highlands*, 104
Gildas, *De Excidio Britanniae*, 6
Glanvilla, Bartholomaeus de, *De Proprietatibus Rerum*, 12, 15
Glasgow, Records of, 34, 37, 42, 70
Gordon of Gordonstoun, Sir Robert, (letter) 39
Gordon of Rothiemay, James, *History of Scots Affair*, 48
Gordon of Straloch, Robert, 42
Gordon, Rachel, (letter) 67
Gordon, Seton, *Highways and Byeways in the West Highlands*, 110
Gordons, MS History of the, 33
Graham, Nicol, 52
Grants, Court Books of the Regality of, 56
Gunn, C. B., *Records of the Baron Court of Stitchill*, 20

Hamilton, Captain, (letter) 56
Harry, Blind, 'Sir William Wallace'. (poem) 15
Heron, R., *Journey Through Scotland*, 104
Hicks, J., *Wandering by the Lochs and Streams*, 107
Hispalensis, Isidorus, *Liber Etymologicarum*, 6
Home, Rev. John, *History of Rebellion of 1745*, 82

Innes of Learney, Sir Thomas, *Tartans of the Clans*, 58
Inveraray Castle Manuscripts, 30
Inverness, Records of, 24, 26, 29, 34, 50

Jacobitism Triumphant, a pamphlet dated 1753, 85

James, Richard, 37
John, Bishop of Glasgow, 15

Keith, George, 10th Earl Marischal, *Memoirs*, 68
Kirk of Scotland, Acts and Proceedings of, 26
Kirke, Thomas, *Account of Scotland*, 49
Kirkhill, Minister of, 43

Lady, The, 109
Lesley, Bishop, *History of Scotland*, 27, 29
Lindsay of Pitscottie, Robert, *History of Scotland*, 20, 26
Lockhart, Bruce, *My Scottish Youth*, 110
Logan, J., *The Scottish Gael*, 106, 107

MacDhonnachaidh Ruaidh, Alasdair, 90
MacDonald of Balshair, Hugh, 109
MacGregor, A. A., *The Turbulent Year*, 108
Mackay, J. G., *Romantic History of the Highland Garb*, 98
MacKenzie, Sir George, *Heraldry*, 44
McKerral, Andrew, 'The Tacksman and his Holding', *Scottish Historical Review*, April 1947, 31
Macky, John, *Journey Through Scotland*, 67
MacPherson of Cluny, Ewan, *Memoirs*, 82
Maitland, John, *History of Edinburgh*, 40
Major, John, *History of Greater Britain*, 12, 19, 20
Martin, Martin, *A Voyage to St. Kilda and Western Isles*, 55, 58
Mason, John, 'Conditions in the Highlands after the Forty-Five', *Scottish Historical Review*, October 1947, 65
Miller, A. E. Haswell, *S.M.T. Magazine*, November, 1947, 46
Moncreiffe of that Ilk, Sir Iain, (footnote) 26
Morer, Rev. Thomas, *A Short Account of Scotland*, 54
Moryson, Fynes, *Itinerary*, 33

Nisbett, Alexander, *System of Heraldry*, 78
Norraboll, Charter of, 30

O'Clery, Peregrine, *Life of Aodh Ruadh O'Donnell*, 33

Patrick, D., *Introduction to the Statutes of the Scottish Church*, 7
Peebles, The Charters of, 16

Pennant, Thomas, *Tour Through Scotland*, 72, 95
Phillip of Almerieclose, James, *The Gramied*, 54
Present State of Scotland, The, 68
Privy Council, Act of, 24

Ramsay, Allan, (poems), 75
Ray, James, *A Complete History of the Rebellion*, 82
Reay, John, *Memorials*, 48
Robertson, R. M., *Angling in Wildest Scotland*, 109
Ronsard, Pierre de, 19

Sacheverell, William, *An Account of the Isle of Man*, 50
St Andrews, Register of Kirk Session, 31
St Andrews, Synodal Statutes of, 12
St Leger, Sir Anthony, 16
Scott, Douglas Hay, *The Badge of Scotland*, 109
Scott, Sir Walter, *Tales of a Grandfather*, 82
Scottish Tourist Board, 112
Shaw, George Bernard, 112
Skenstone, W., 'Jemmy Dawson', (ballad) 85
Skinner, Rev. John, (poem) 75
Slezer, Captain John, *Theatrum Scotiae*, 55
Smollett, Tobias, *Humphrey Clinker*, 90
Spenser, Edmund, *View of the Present State of Ireland*, 16
Statistical Account of Scotland 1793, 52, 78, 92, 95, 96, 103
Stevenson, R. L., *Virginibus Puerisque*, 108
Stuart brothers, *Vestiarium Scoticum*, 30
'Sym and his Bruder', (poem) 26

Tacitus, Cornelius, *De Vita Iulii Agricolae*, 6
Taylor, John, *The Pennylesse Pilgrimage*, 37, 39
Terry, C. S., *History of Scotland*, 7
Tisdall, E. E. P., *Queen Victoria's John Brown*, 108
Turgot, Bishop of St Andrews, *Life of St Margaret*, 7

Wardlaw, MS, 43
Webster, David, *Topographical Dictionary of Scotland*, 106
Wedderburne, David, (accounts) 33, 37
William of Malmesbury, *Gesta Regum Anglorum*, 6

Young, John, 16